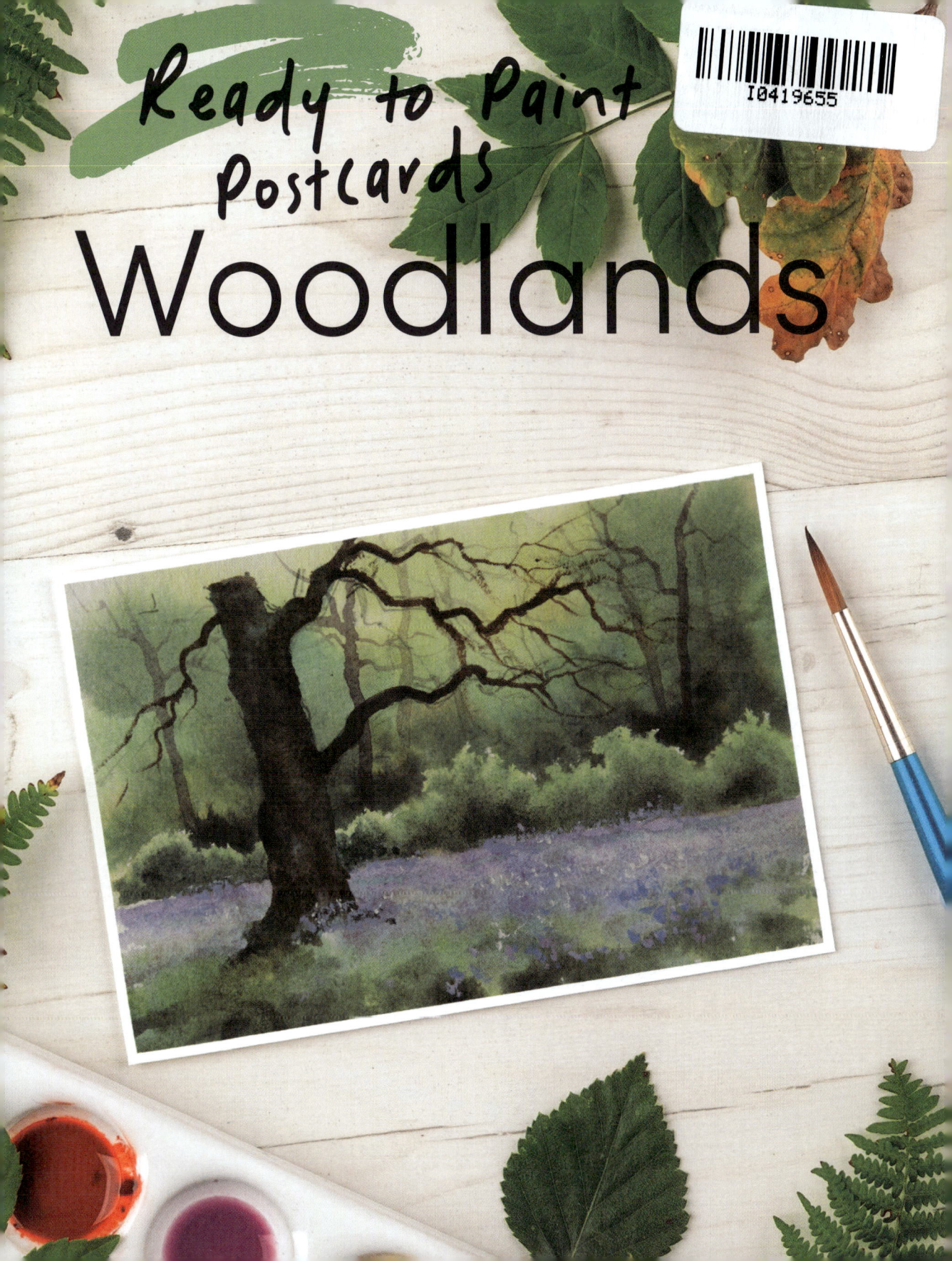

Ready to Paint
Postcards
Woodlands

First published in 2025
Search Press Limited
Wellwood, North Farm Road,
Tunbridge Wells, Kent TN2 3DR
Text copyright © Geoff Kersey, 2018, 2025
Photographs by Roddy Paine Photographic Studios
Photographs and design copyright © Search Press Ltd. 2025

This book contains material previously published as *Ready to Paint in 30 Minutes: Trees and Woodlands*, 2018

ISBN: 978-1-80092-295-2
ebook ISBN: 978-1-80093-286-9

Bookmarked Hub
Extra copies of the outline drawings are also available to download free from the Bookmarked Hub. Search for this book by title or ISBN: the files can be found under 'Book Extras'. Membership of the Bookmarked online community is free: www.bookmarkedhub.com

Publishers' note
The Publishers and author can accept no responsibility for any consequences arising from the information, advice or instructions given in this publication.

Readers are permitted to reproduce any of the projects in this book for their personal use, or for the purpose of selling for charity, free of charge and without the prior permission of the Publishers. You are not permitted to use any of the projects or artworks for commercial purposes, or for the purpose of training artificial intelligence technologies or systems.

We do our best to ensure that all of our books are error-free. If you spot anything that's not quite right, check on our website (www.searchpress.com) or the Bookmarked Hub (www.bookmarkedhub.com) to find any mistakes we've already fixed.

MIX
Paper | Supporting
responsible forestry
FSC® C144853

Ready to Paint Postcards

Woodlands

15 stunning watercolour paintings to create in just 30 minutes

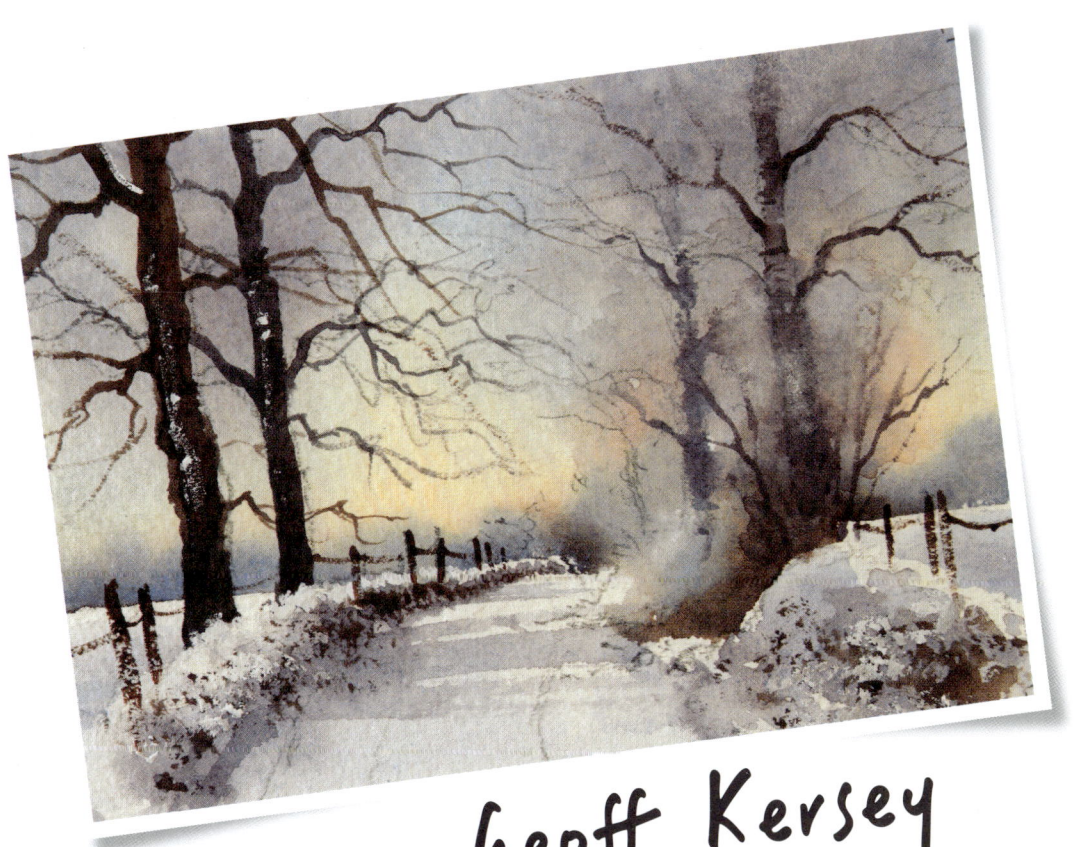

Geoff Kersey

SEARCH PRESS

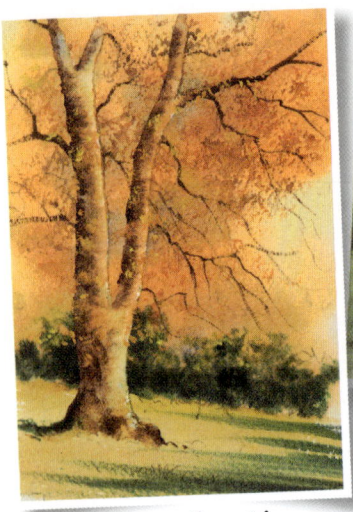

Autumn Tree 16

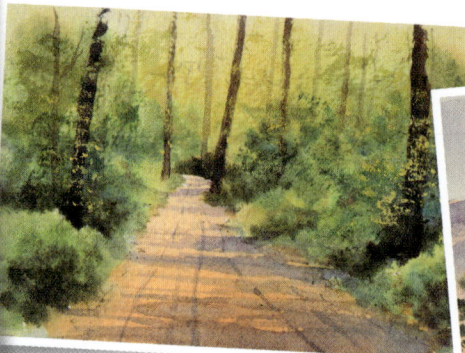

Spring Trees 22

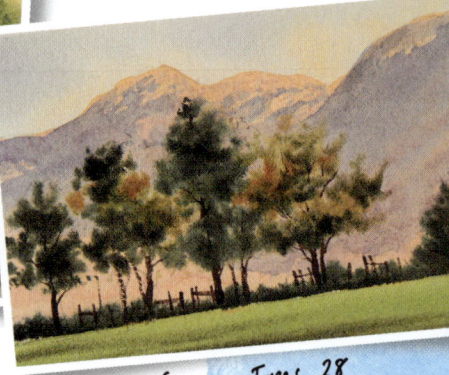

Summer Trees 28

Contents

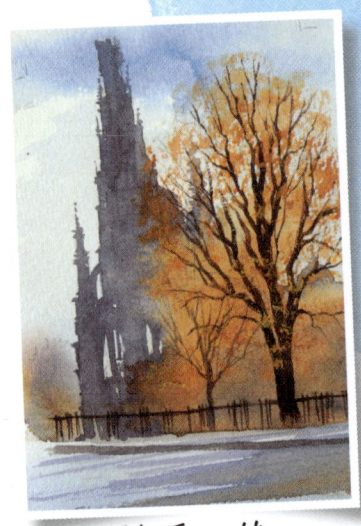

City Trees 44

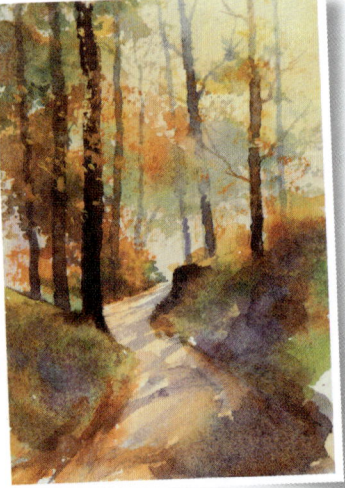

Dappled Sunlight 62

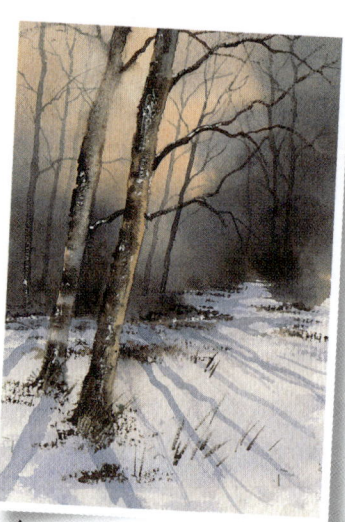

Looking into the Light 68

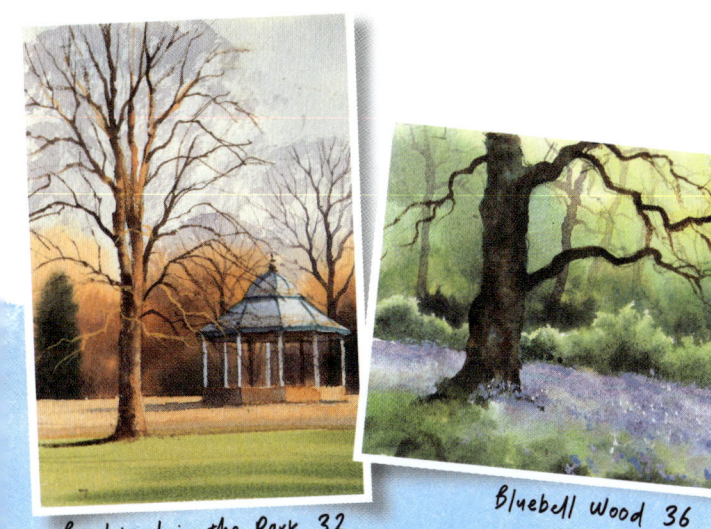

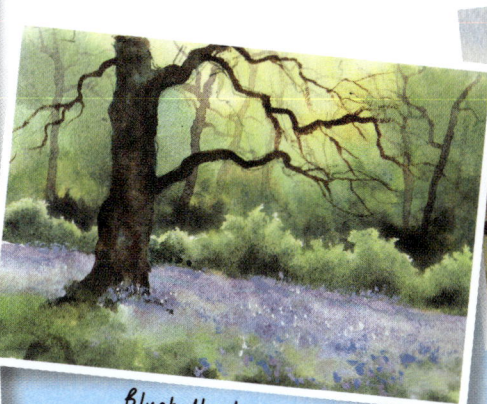

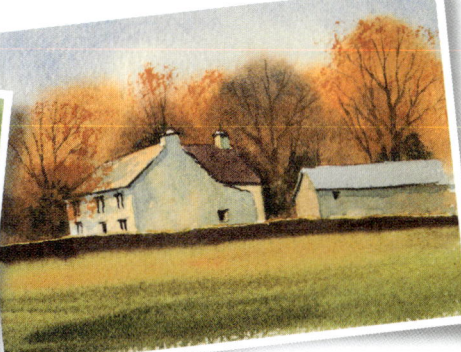

Farmhouse 40

Bandstand in the Park 32

Bluebell Wood 36

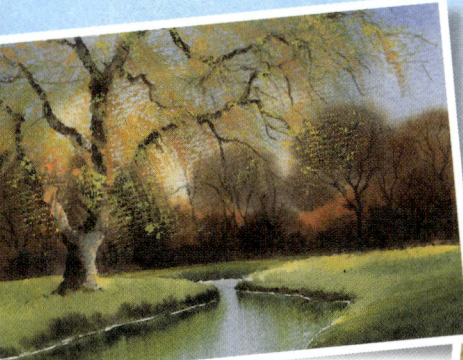

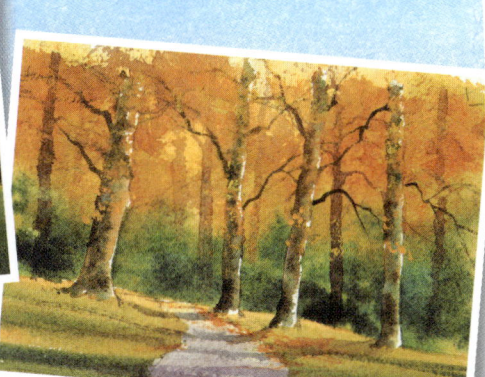

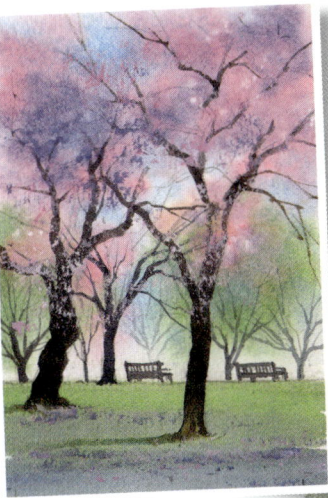

Weeping Willow 48

Cherry Blossom 56

Parkland in Autumn 52

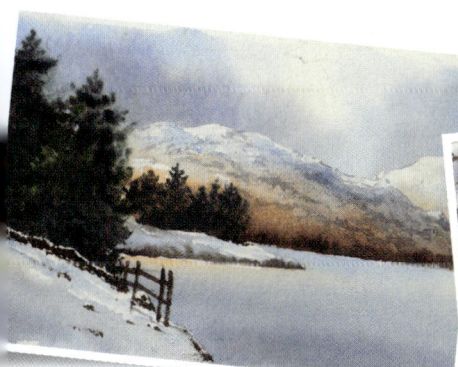

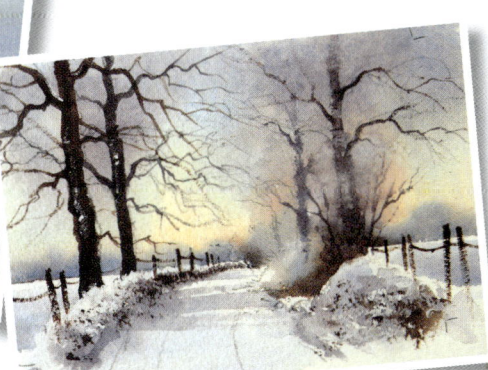

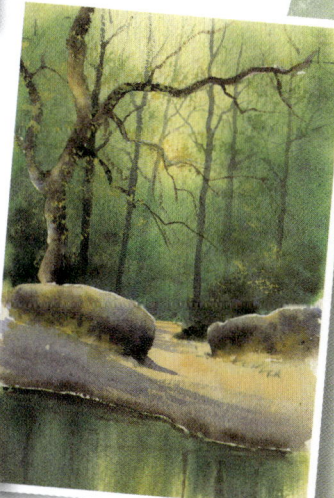

Fir Trees 72

Winter Lane 76

Pond Reflections 80

Introduction

The short projects in this book are designed to be painted in just half an hour on postcard-sized – that is, 15 x 10cm (6 x 4in) – sheets of watercolour paper. However, don't regard this as a strict time limit. If you take a little longer, that's fine: the aim is to make a statement with your brush and paint over a short period, then enjoy the freshness of the result. You will be surprised what can be achieved in the time.

It is possible, even likely, that not every postcard will work out exactly as you hope, but as half an hour of painting is relatively easy to fit into even a busy day, you can give the project another go by re-using the outline drawings, which can be found at the back of the book.

I wanted to include enough variety and interest in these postcard paintings to be useful to any aspiring artist, so the postcards include trees as part of a variety of landscape scenes. Some feature buildings or natural phenomena like rocks and geological structures, some look at individual trees, while others offer woodlands as a mass of foliage.

By working through the projects, you will create a collection of fifteen small, complete postcard paintings, each of which covers a different technique or subject on the theme of trees and woodlands. By the end of the book, you will find you have built up your skills and are ready to tackle more complex, involved projects.

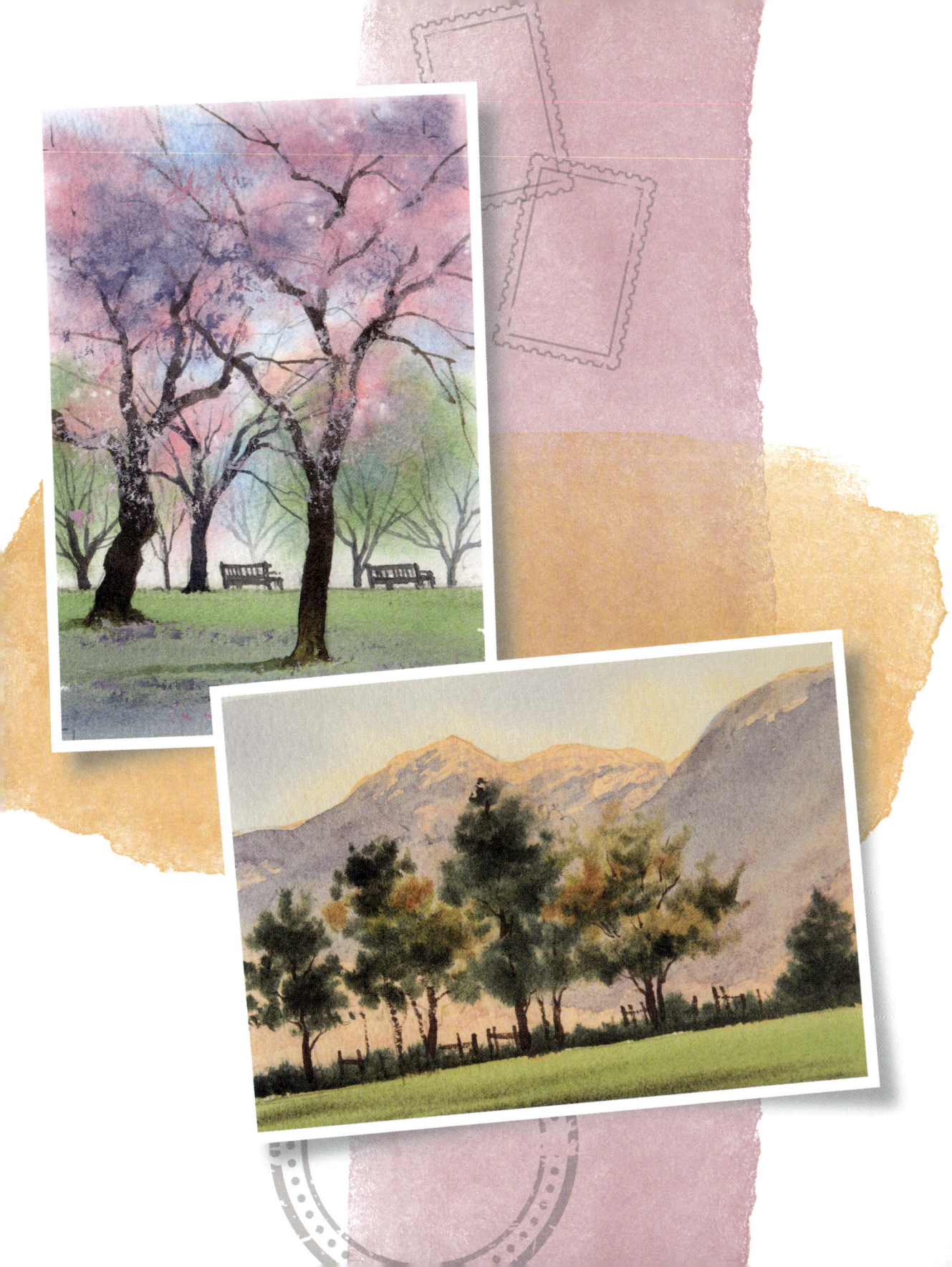

Watercolour basics

Whether you have used watercolours before or not, it's worth taking half an hour to get to grips with your tools and learn a few fundamental painting techniques before moving on.

You'll find additional techniques dotted throughout the book, so if you work through from the start, you'll find your skills build naturally as you go on.

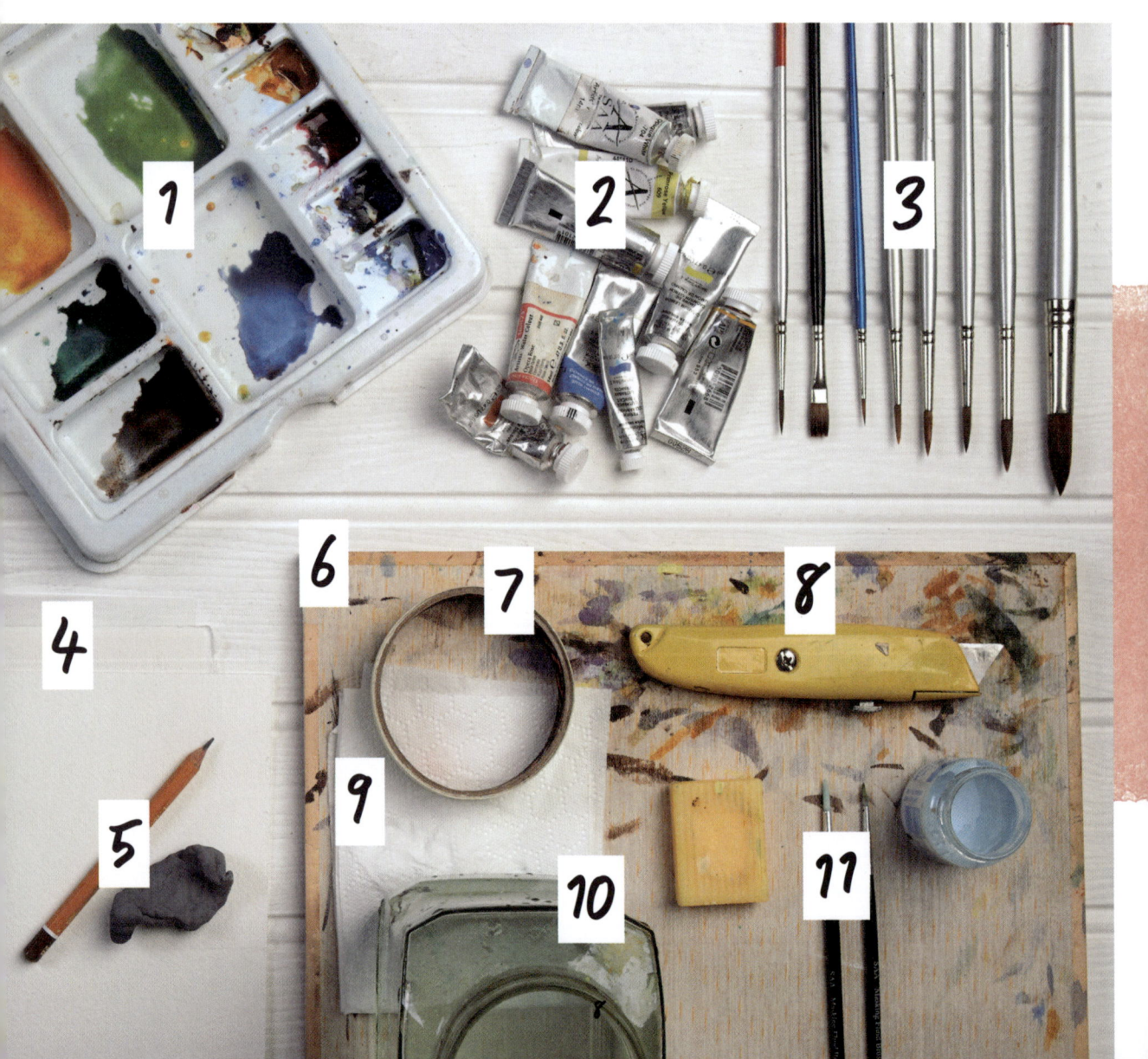

Basic painting equipment

1 Palette My palette is plastic with small wells for the fresh paint and large mixing areas. It has a lid and a sponge membrane which is dampened to keep the paint moist and workable between painting sessions.

2 Paints I use tube colour exclusively (as opposed to pans) as it is much easier to mix. I prefer artists' quality paint to students' quality as their greater proportion of pigment to gum means that artists' range paints go further. I recommend larger 14ml tubes, which are very economical.

3 Brushes I prefer the springy nature of synthetic brushes; and find natural hair brushes to be too absorbent and difficult to control. I use mainly round brushes, having a number 2, 4, 6, 8, 10 and 16 in my collection, together with 12mm (½in) and 25mm (1in) flat brushes. I also use a liner/writer for very fine work, like tree branches and long grasses.

4 Paper The paper you use has the biggest impact on the finished product, so go for good-quality rag-based watercolour paper. The outline drawings and projects are designed for a postcard-sized (15 x 10cm/6 x 4in) pad of paper. My favourite papers are Saunders Waterford's Rough surface, and Arches Not (or Cold-Pressed) surface. I prefer a heavier 640gsm (300lb) paper as this avoids cockling when the paper becomes wet, and does not need stretching.

5 Pencil and eraser I draw the subject prior to applying paint with a 2B, 0.9 mechanical pencil, and use a 0.7 for finer detail. These have the advantage of not needing constant sharpening. Use a putty eraser to remove or fade pencil lines.

6 Painting board 12mm (½in) plywood works well to support the painting while you work. I also recommend the lightweight drawing boards commercially available.

7 Masking tape Most often used to hold the paper in position, this can also be used to mask out the edges, creating a mount effect around the edge of the painting.

8 Craft knife This is mainly used for cutting paper and scratching out effects.

9 Kitchen paper I always have a roll standing by to mop up accidents. It can also be used sparingly to create texture, by dabbing on the damp colour.

10 Water pot Any large pot can be used, but rinse it out regularly to ensure your supply of water remains clean.

11 Masking fluid, brushes and soap Masking fluid protects areas that you want to keep as crisp, clean white paper. Use cheaper brushes to apply the masking fluid, as they will get 'gummed up'.

Filling your palette

Each postcard painting is accompanied by a list of paint colours that you will need. Before you start, gently squeeze a small amount of each paint into one of the small wells in your palette, as shown to the right.

As you work, try to keep your colours clean to avoid muddying your paints. Use a clean brush to pick up pure paint from the palette well, and always mix in a larger mixing well, as shown opposite. If you do end up accidentally introducing another colour into a well, you can wipe the whole well clean and start again.

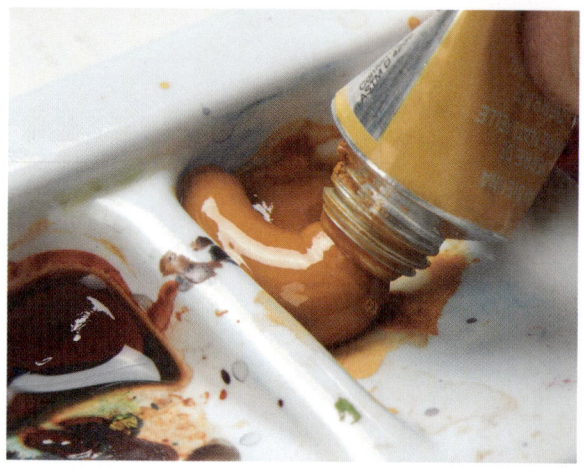

Watercolour goes a long way and can be expensive, so there's no need to squeeze out huge amounts – better to start with a small amount and add more to your palette well as you need it.

Choosing and using brushes

It may be tempting to try to use tiny brushes to get control over the paint, but this will result in a fussy, overly textural finish. Larger brushes hold more paint, so they allow you to create the smooth, luminous washes (see page 12) that are so attractive in watercolour.

As a general rule, larger brushes are used for larger areas like skies (see right); while small brushes are reserved for finer details (see below right). As with the paint colours, the brushes you need for an project are listed at the start and explained in the text accompanying each step.

Be sure to rinse your brushes thoroughly in clean water between using different mixes of paint – this is a most important point to make, as you will get dirty, muddy mixes by swapping between colours without cleaning your brush.

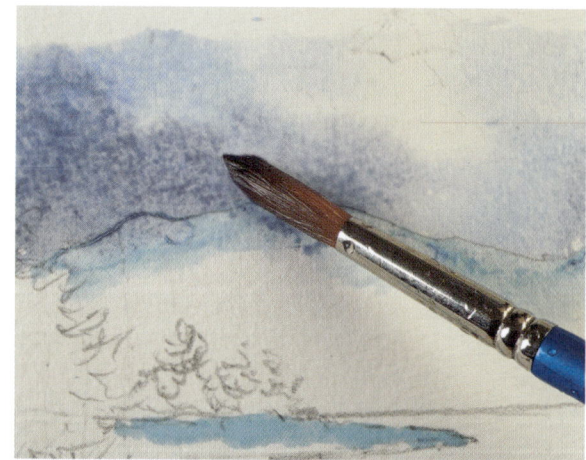

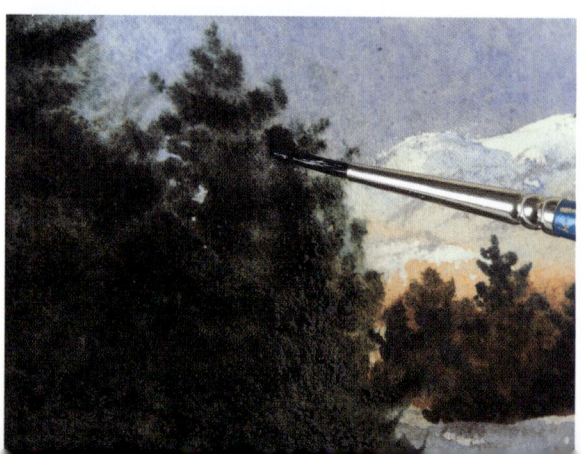

Preparing your paint

When preparing paint, use a wet brush to pick up the paint from the well, then deposit it in one of your larger mixing wells. You can then add more pigment, or more water to the mixing well to adjust the fluidity of the paint as shown in the steps below – don't start with a pool of clean water.

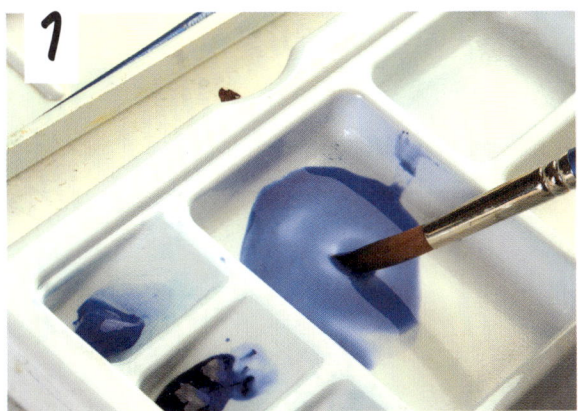

▶ Prepare your paint by wetting your brush and picking up some paint from your palette. Transfer it to a clean well, then pick up clean water on the brush and add it to the well. Stir it gently to ensure the paint and water mix, but there is no need to scrub.

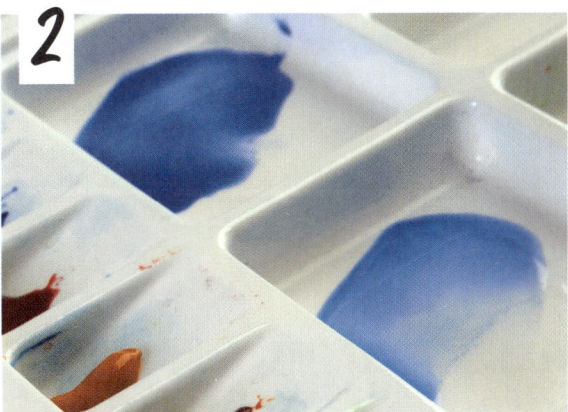

▶ You can add more water to dilute the paint further and help you create lighter tints; or more pigment to create darker, deeper colour.

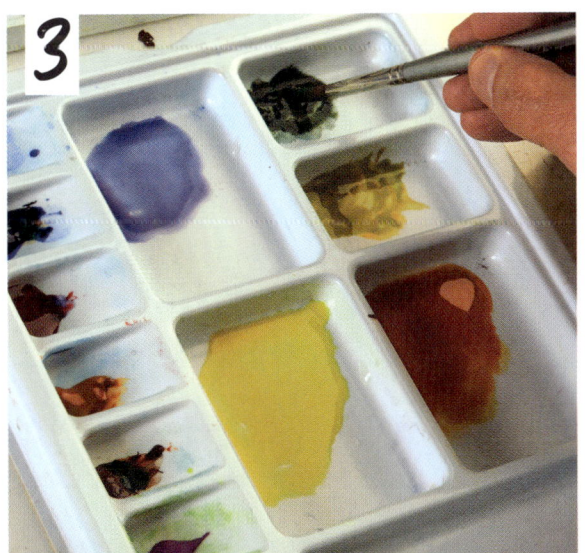

▶ That's it! The only other thing to remember is that you can combine colours to create new mixes; this is part of the skill of watercolour painting. All you need do is add a different paint to the mixing area and stir it gently into the first.

Washes and consistency

Most watercolour painting involves the application of washes. A wash is a thin, fluid mixture of paint and water, roughly the consistency of skimmed milk. Watercolour washes dry slightly lighter than they appear when wet, so take this into account when preparing them.

You will also need to use some thicker paint mixes for the postcard paintings in this book, but even these are still diluted with a little clean water to help them flow smoothly. Make such mixes thicker than washes; each should be akin to full cream milk.

In a few rare cases, noted within each project, you may need to apply neat watercolour or gouache.

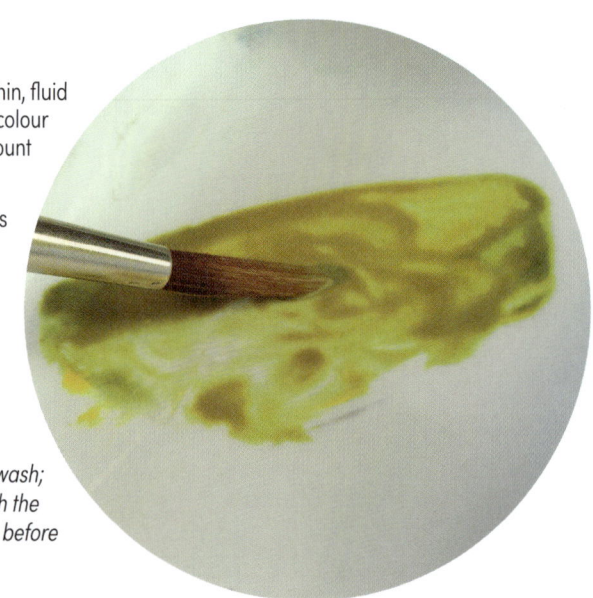

This green mix is slightly less dilute than a wash; you can see how the movements made with the brush remain apparent for a few moments before the paint flows back, flat and even.

TECHNIQUE: APPLYING A WASH WET-IN-WET

Wet-in-wet refers to adding wet colour onto still-wet paint. This allows the colours to bleed and blend together. You need to work fairly quickly to ensure the paint on the surface does not have time to dry before you apply the next colours.

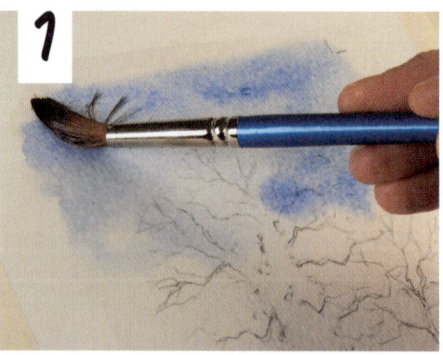

▶ Prepare a dilute well of paint. Wet the area where you want the wash to be, using clean water and the size 16 round. Pick up some of the colour and drop the paint in across the top of the wet area.

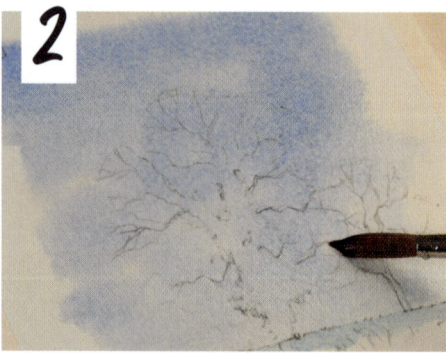

▶ Work downwards. While the paint remains wet, rinse your brush and squeeze it gently to remove excess water. Gently touch it to the paint near to the horizon to lift away some wet paint and create a mottled, lighter effect to suggest clouds on the horizon. Rinse and squeeze the brush and repeat.

TECHNIQUE: DRY BRUSH

The dry brush technique relies on catching the raised texture of the paper surface. It works best with less dilute paint, on a Not or Rough surface paper.

Hold the brush as shown below left. This allows you to get the whole side of the brush on the paper, rather than just the tip. As a result, when you lightly stroke it across, you miss the indentations of the textured paper surface and only hit the raised parts, creating a broken, leafy effect.

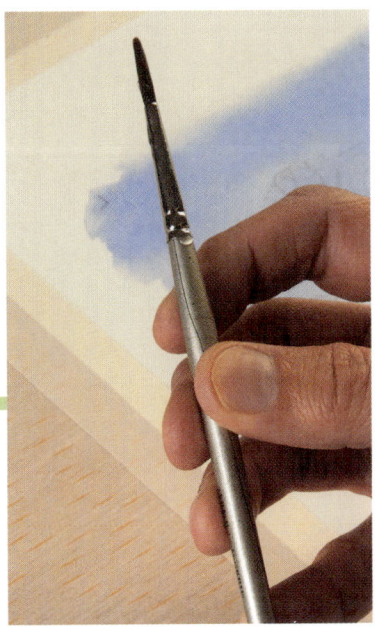

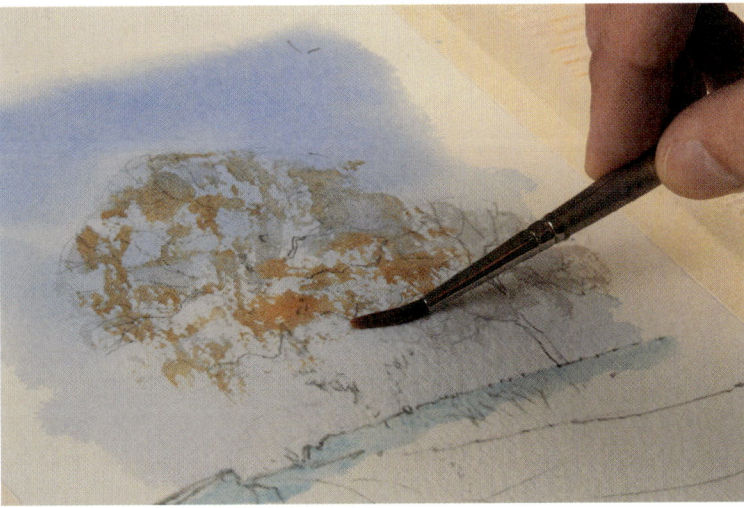

It is important that your brush is not too wet for this technique, or the paint will flow into the recesses of the textured surface and spoil the effect. Be careful not to press too hard, either – the brush should skim the surface of the paper.

Using masking fluid

Masking fluid allows you to preserve the white surface of the paper. It's important to know both how to apply it, and how to remove the fluid cleanly, too.

Masking fluid needs to be applied in a certain way to ensure that it properly protects the surface – and to avoid damage to your brush. If it dries in the bristles of the brush, it cannot be removed. You should use a specific brush for applying masking fluid – either an old brush or a brush specifically set aside for applying the fluid.

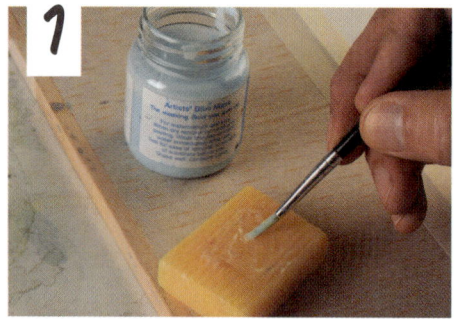

▶ Dampen the brush and rub it on a bar of soap to act as a barrier before dipping it in the masking fluid, and the brush will last longer.

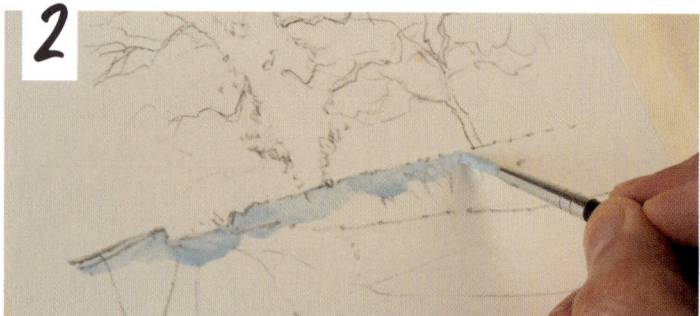

▶ Use the brush to apply the masking fluid just like paint. Anything under the masking fluid will be protected from the paint and remain clean until the masking fluid is rubbed away later. Allow the masking fluid to dry before continuing.

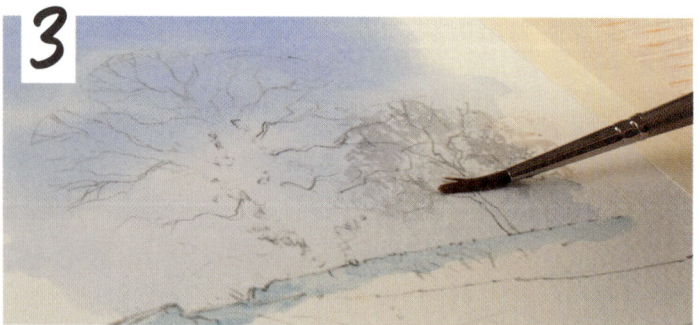

▶ It's now safe to paint up to and over the area of masking fluid.

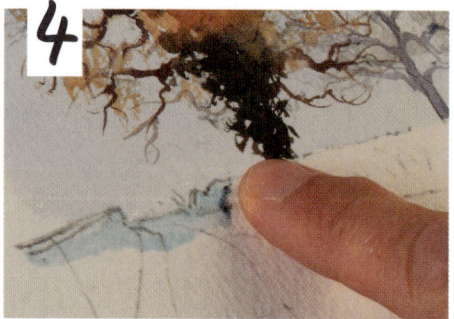

▶ Once the paint is dry, use a clean finger to gently rub away the masking fluid. It will lift away fairly easily, revealing a crisp edge on the clean paper underneath.

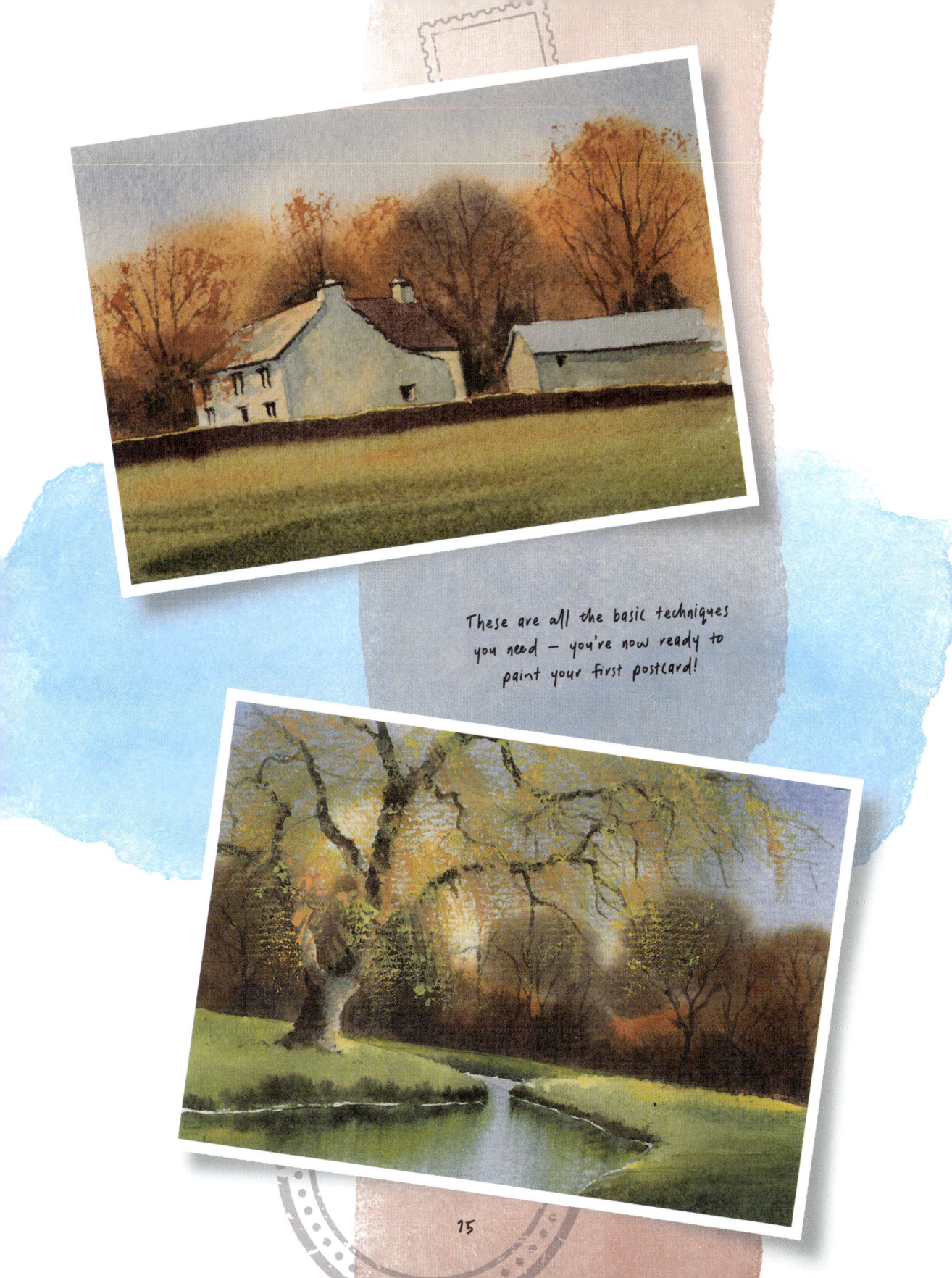

These are all the basic techniques you need — you're now ready to paint your first postcard!

Autumn Tree

This project introduces the variegated wash, which allows you to quickly and easily create an interesting variation in colour across an area. As demonstrated here, it is perfect for describing the texture and complexity of distant foliage, but it has many applications more generally.

YOU WILL NEED

Paint colours: cobalt blue, rose madder, lemon yellow, aureolin, burnt sienna, viridian, French ultramarine

Brushes: masking fluid brush, size 16 round, size 10 round, size 8 round, size 2 round, size 6 round, size 4 round

Other: masking fluid, bar of soap, outline drawing on page 85

TECHNIQUE: VARIEGATED WASH

This technique creates a varied mix of colours that is fantastic for suggesting distant, slightly out-of-focus foliage; perfect for trees and woodlands.

1

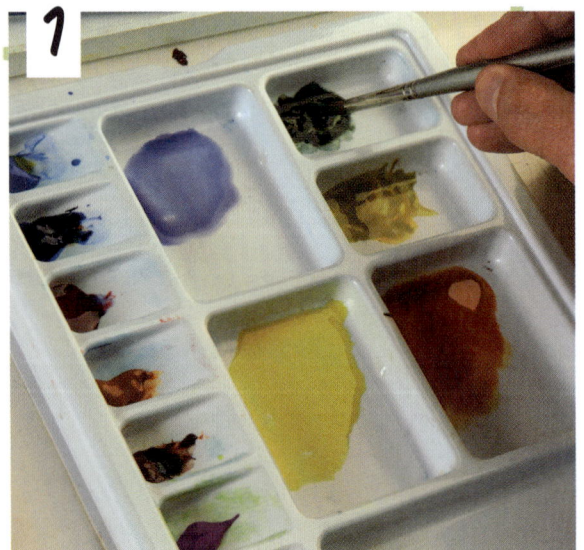

▶ Mask the trunk and main branches of the large tree; ignore the smaller branches (see step 2). As the masking dries, make a thin purple wash of cobalt blue and rose madder; a thin wash of lemon yellow; a lightly thicker orange mix for autumn foliage from aureolin and burnt sienna; a bright green wash from aureolin and cobalt blue; and finally a dark green from viridian, French ultramarine and burnt sienna.

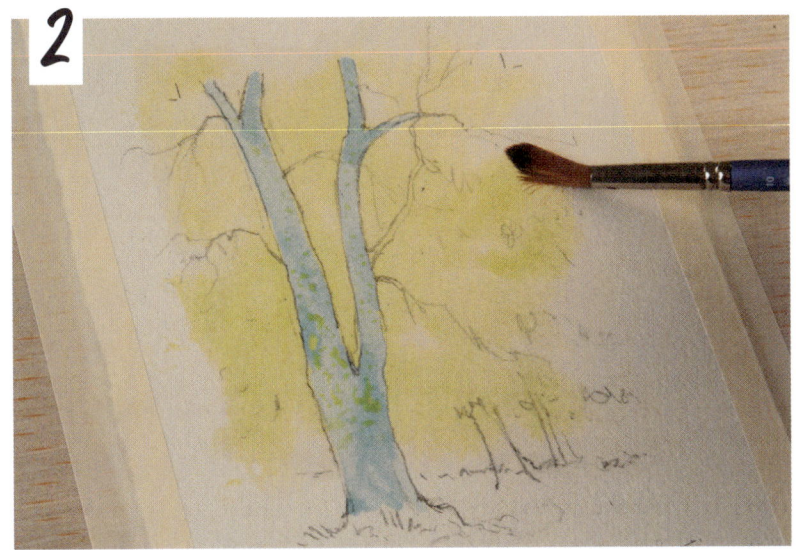

▶ Wet the whole of the background with clean water and the size 16 round brush, except for the forest floor. Look for the shine on the paper to ensure you have covered everything, then paint the wet area with your first colour – lemon yellow in this case.

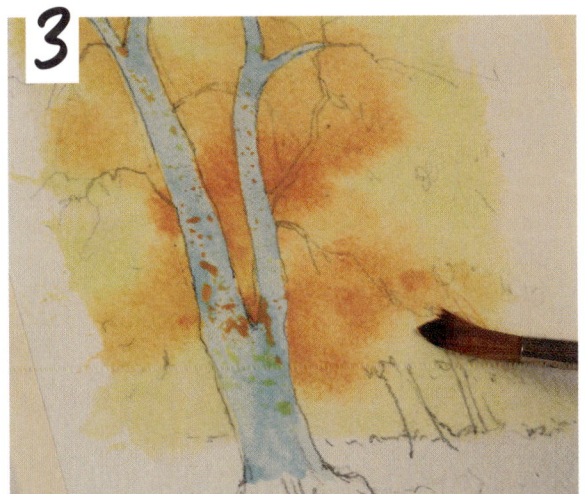

▶ Working wet-in-wet and using the same brush, add the other colours (the autumn foliage and orange mixes) here and there, letting them bleed into the existing paint.

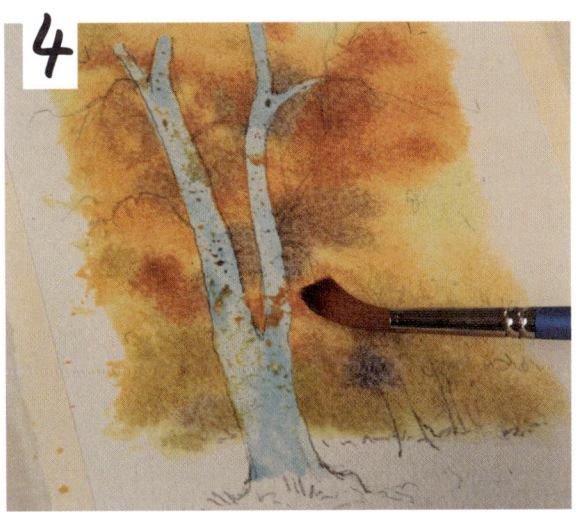

▶ Add a little of the purple mix near the tree, then add the bright green around the bottom of the area.

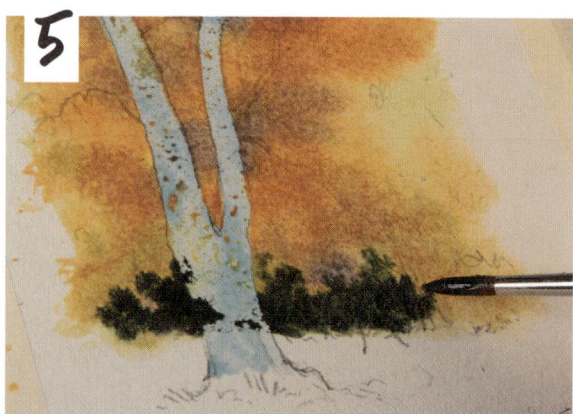

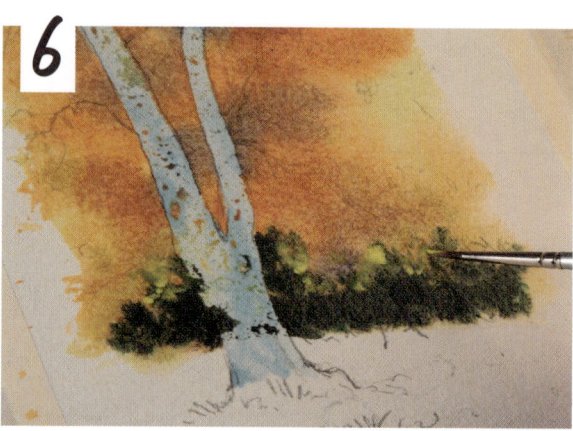

▶ Add darker touches around the tree using the size 8 and the dark green mix (viridian, French ultramarine and burnt sienna), applying the paint with the tip of the brush and letting the paint soften in – if you time it correctly, the paint will largely do the work for you. If it starts to run away out of control, wait a moment for the background to dry a little before trying again.

▶ Pick up some pure lemon yellow – either from the tube or from your palette well – and touch in some highlights at the top of the dark area with the tip of the size 2 brush.

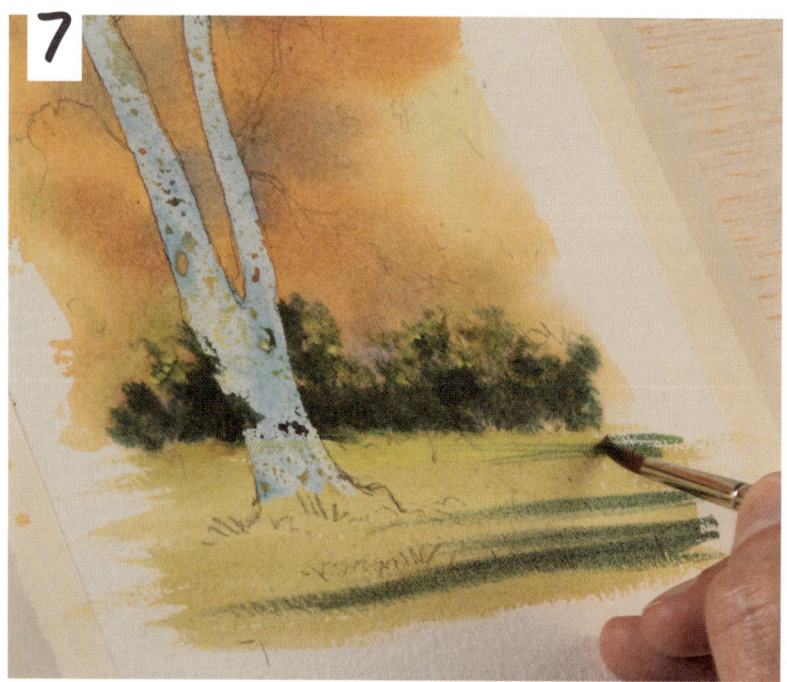

▶ Change to the size 10 round and use long sweeping strokes to paint the grasses in the foreground with the bright green mix (aureolin and cobalt blue). Paint beyond the edges of the picture, to ensure you fill it evenly. Add some aureolin highlights, then change to the size 6 brush and add shadows with the dark green mix; again making fairly horizontal strokes.

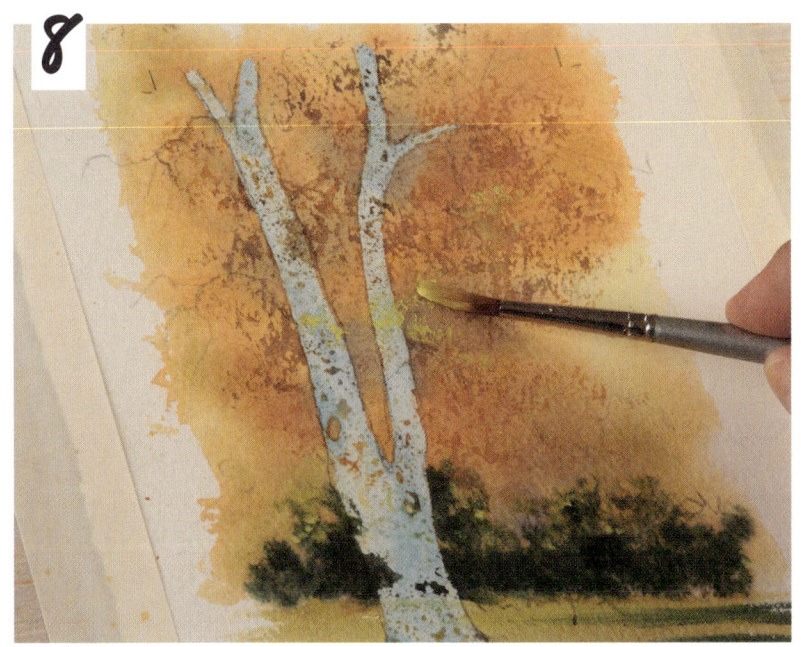

8

▶ Once it has dried, use the dry brush technique to paint over the main branches of the tree with the orange mix (aureolin and burnt sienna) and then the purple mix (cobalt blue and rose madder). This will create masses of leaves quickly and without having to paint each leaf individually. Add some sunlit leaves in the same way using lemon yellow. Once dry, use a clean finger to remove the masking fluid.

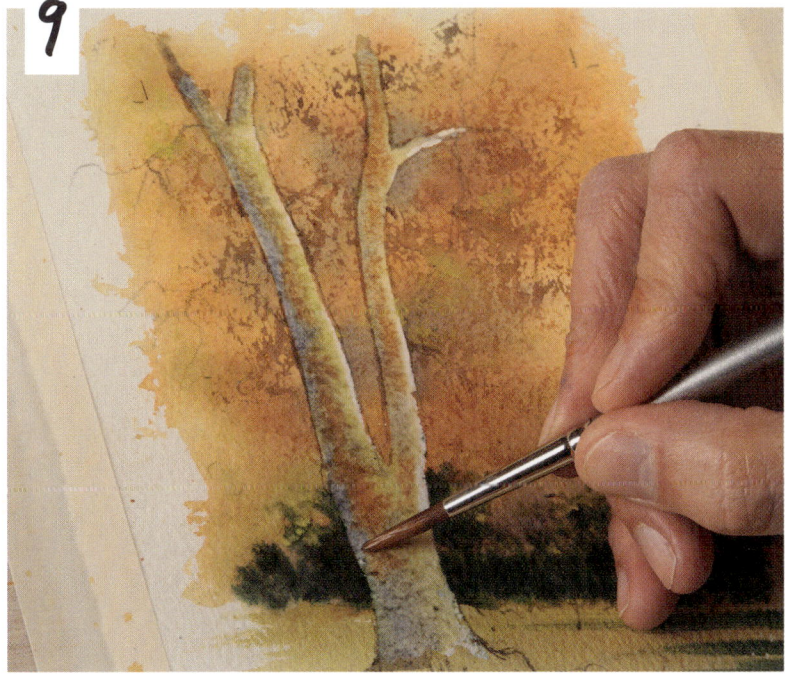

9

▶ Wet the whole tree with clean water, using the size 6 round, then build up a variegated wash by adding the bright green mix, very diluted. While wet, add touches of the purple mix and orange mix here and there.

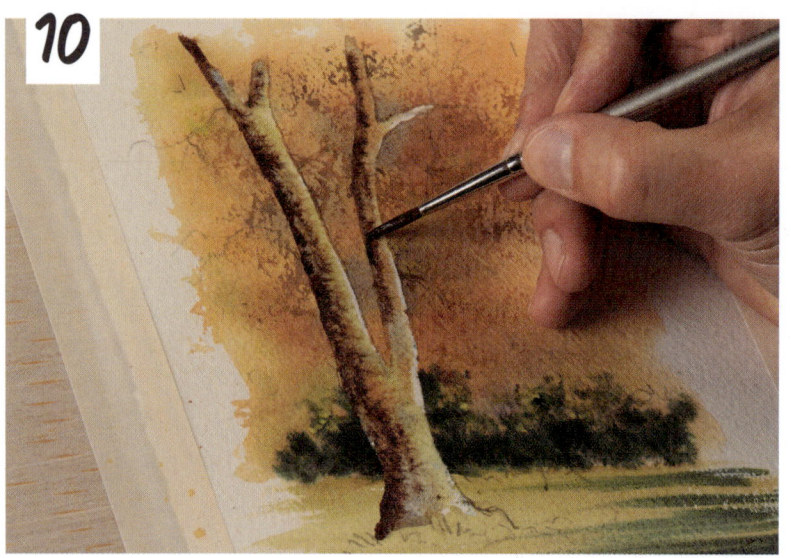

10

▶ In order to make the tree look cylindrical, add stronger, darker tones on one side as shadows. Use the size 4 to add a dark mix of burnt sienna and French ultramarine wet-in-wet. Do not aim for a clean effect, or the tree will look unnatural, like a pipe. Adding a little texture makes it appear weathered and naturalistic. Add some very light-toned colour – lemon yellow – on the opposite side as a highlight.

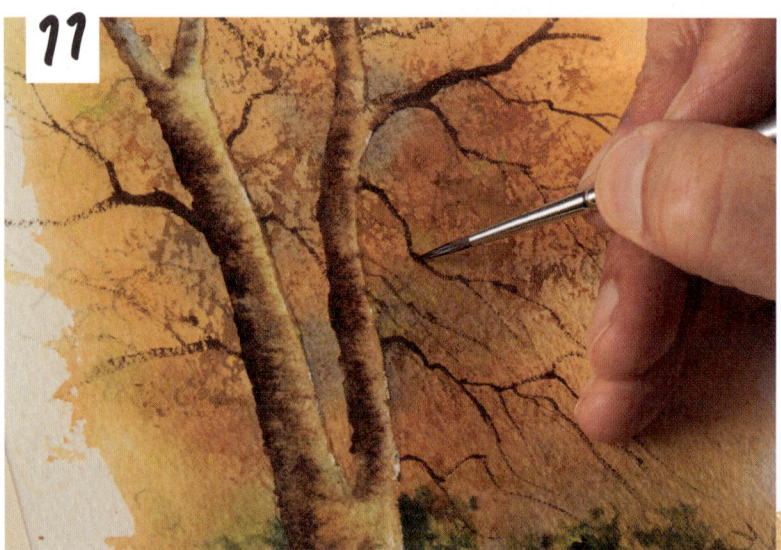

11

▶ Change to the size 2 round brush and the dark mix to paint in the finer branches, working outwards from the trunk and lifting it away to create a tapering, fine effect.

FINISHING TOUCHES

To finish the painting, a mix of neat lemon yellow and burnt sienna can be worked over the surface using the size 4 round brush and the dry brush technique to create the impression of leaves in front of the trunk. Add a few small dashes – not dots, which can look unnatural – of the same mix to create a few individual leaves in the foreground with the size 2 brush. Anchor the tree to the ground by using the same mixes as the trunk to soften it into the dry grass area, then use the dark mix to create a shadow on the left-hand side.

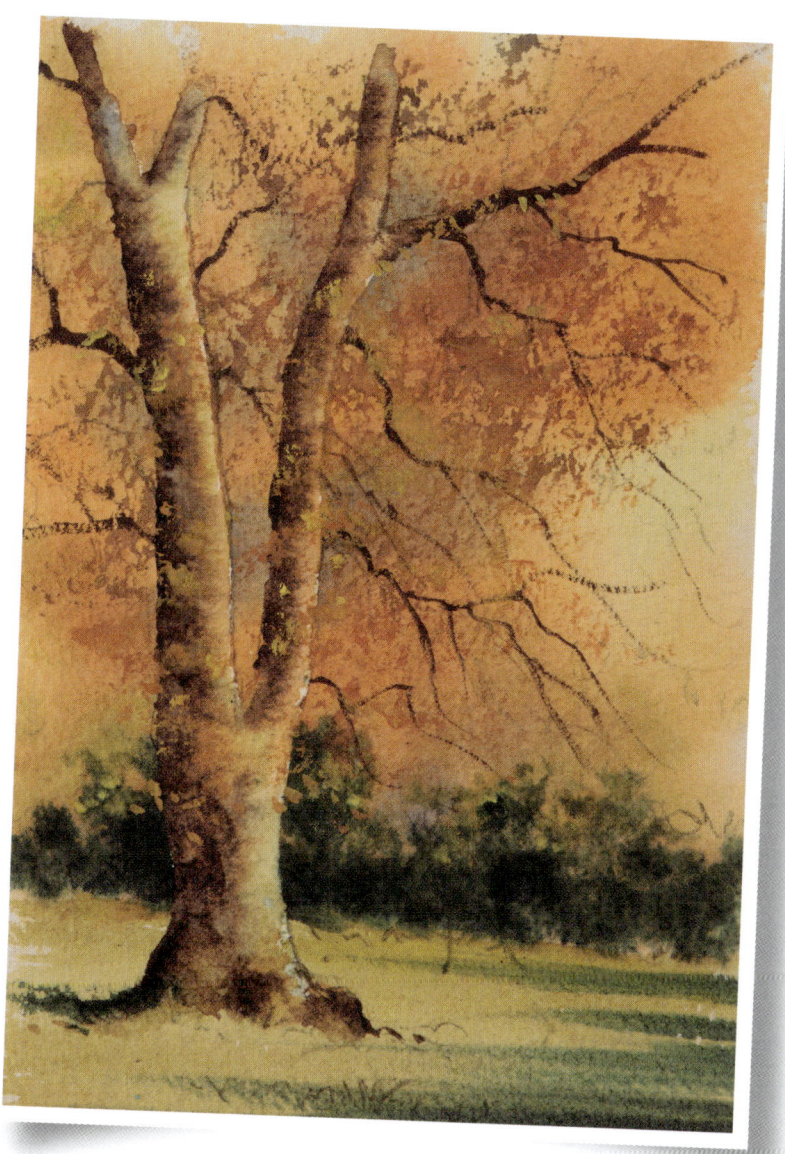

The finished postcard

Spring Trees

This project introduces feathered masking, a technique that allows you to use masking fluid that flows a little like paint in order to achieve soft edges. Once dry, this will help to create a soft, feathered edge to the area, rather than the usual hard edge. It also introduces the use of body colour – opaque paint, which enables us to paint over the top of existing work: very useful for certain effects. The paint used in this example, primrose yellow, is essentially lemon yellow with a touch of white gouache added, so you can mix a version of it yourself if you cannot find the premixed primrose yellow.

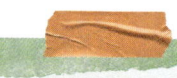

YOU WILL NEED

Paint colours: lemon yellow, aureolin, cobalt blue, viridian, French ultramarine, burnt sienna, cerulean blue, cobalt violet

Brushes: masking fluid brush, size 16 round, size 10 round, size 8 round, size 2 round, size 6 round, size 4 round

Other: masking fluid, bar of soap, primrose yellow body colour, outline drawing on page 86 (top)

TECHNIQUE: FEATHERED MASKING

This technique avoids the hard lines that masking fluid normally leaves, instead creating a softer effect. Be careful to wet more than you need – once the masking fluid reaches the edge of the water, you'll get a hard edge: just what you're trying to avoid.

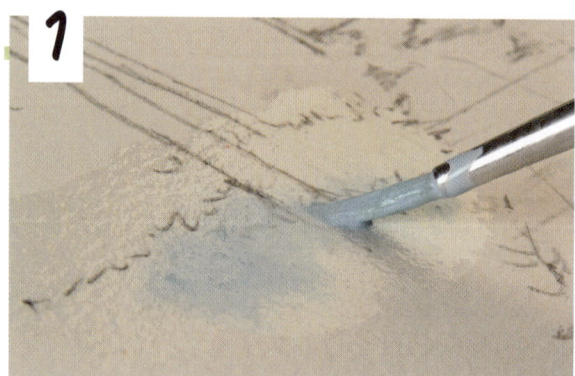

▶ Wet the area around where you want to mask – in this case around the base of the tree. While wet, use the masking fluid brush to drop in masking fluid as normal.

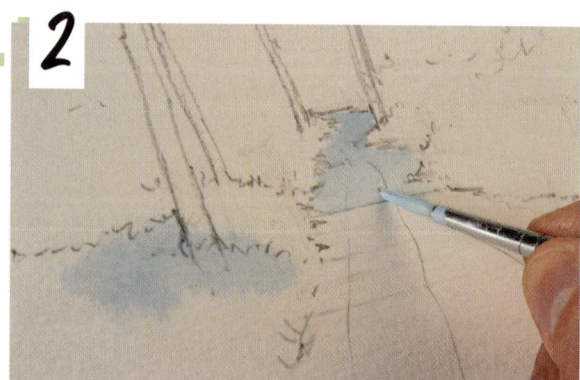

▶ Mask the path as normal for masking (see page 14) before continuing. This will help to illustrate the difference in effect later.

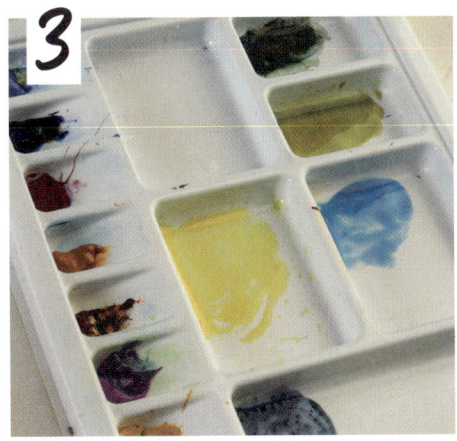

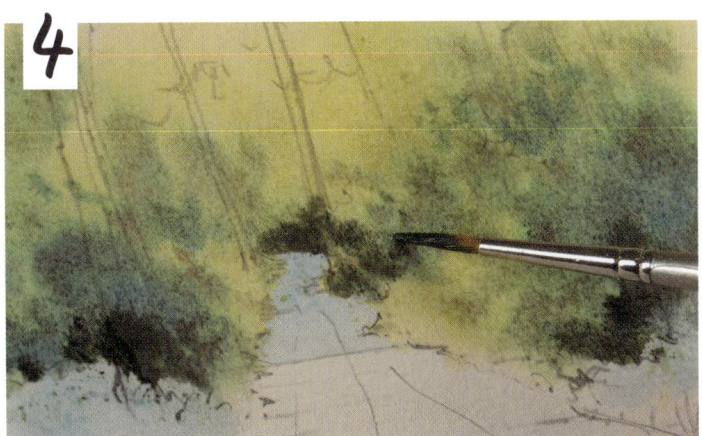

▶ While the masking fluid dries, prepare your colours. Make a thin wash of lemon yellow; a thicker bright green mix of aureolin and cobalt blue; a dark green mix of viridian, French ultramarine and burnt sienna; a wash of cerulean blue; and a green-grey mix of viridian and cobalt violet.

▶ Wet the whole of the background – not the path or foreground – with clean water using the size 16 brush. Make a variegated wash over the area by laying in lemon yellow with the side of the size 10 brush, then add touches of the bright green mix, then the grey-green mix. Keep the grey-green mix towards the bottom of the area, and work right down to – and onto – the masking fluid. Change to the size 6 round brush and add some cerulean blue touches while the paint remains wet. Finally, change to the size 4 round and paint in denser areas of foliage with the dark green mix. Add these near the areas of masking fluid – this will create maximum contrast with the white of the paper when the masking fluid is later removed.

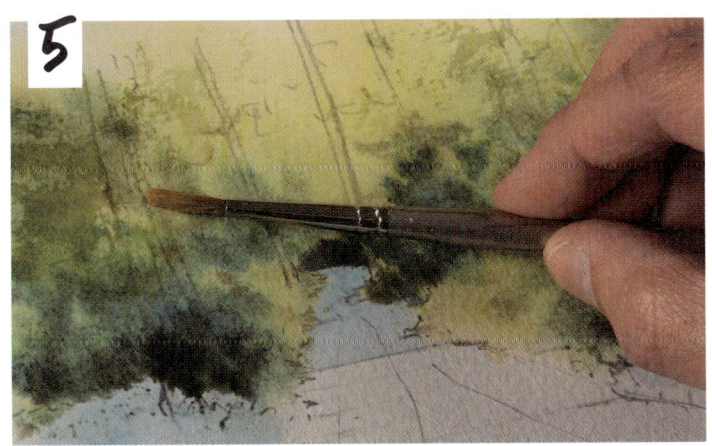

▶ Once dry, break up the foliage with the dry brush technique (see page 13) and the brighter colours – the lemon yellow and the thicker bright green mix.

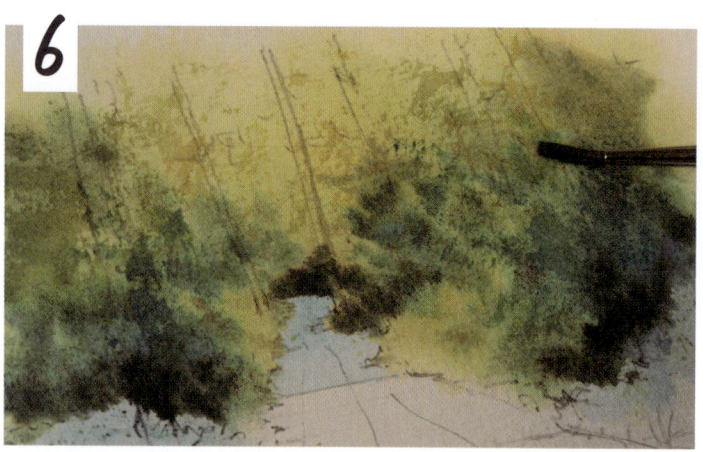

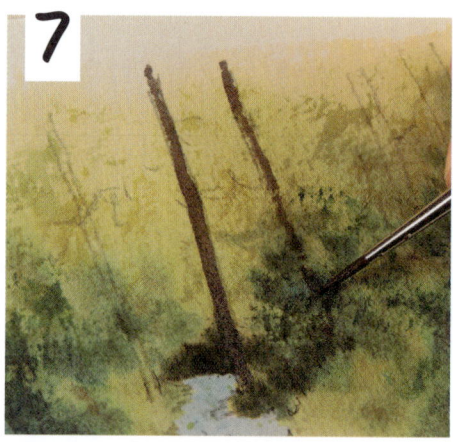

▶ Continue building up the texture in the foliage using the medium-toned and dark-toned mixes (aureolin and cobalt blue; and viridian, French ultramarine and burnt sienna respectively) with the dry brush technique. Be more sparing with the darker tones than the lighter ones; be careful not to cover the brighter touches you have just added. Do not overwork this dry brush technique: keep stopping and asking yourself whether you have done enough.

▶ Use the size 2 round brush to paint in the midground trees using the grey-green mix (viridian and cobalt violet). Start from the bottom and work up each trunk in turn, breaking up the line near the bottom to suggest intervening foliage.

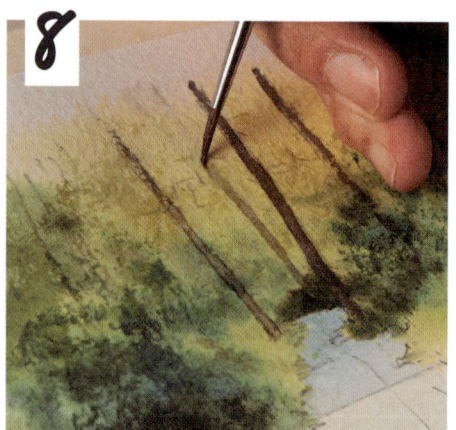

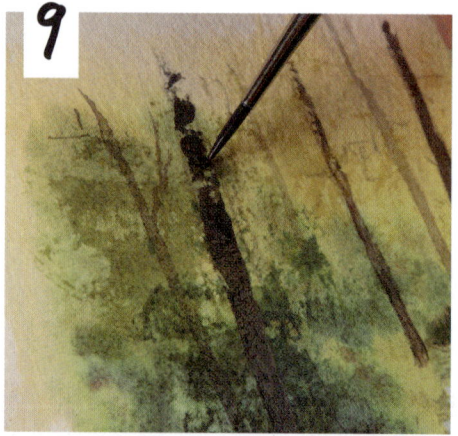

▶ Dilute the mix to soften it, and paint in some more trees. Those painted with more dilute paint will appear more distant. The lighter tone creates the illusion of depth in the painting.

▶ Similarly, strengthening the tone, by adding more paint, will allow you to paint trees that appear closer. These will be more convincing if you paint them a little larger than the midground trees and allow the drier paint to break up a little, as this will create the impression of more detail and intervening leaves.

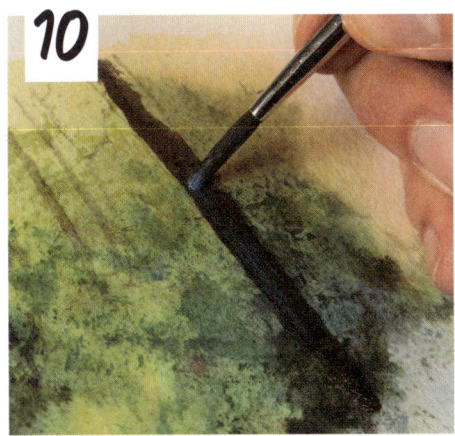

▶ Brush some neat cerulean blue with the size 4 round into the darker, nearer trees to prevent them being too oppressive.

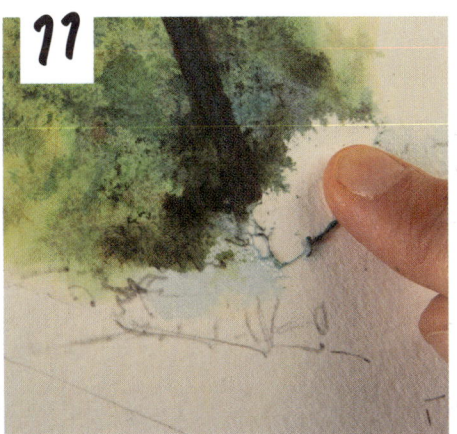

▶ Once dry, carefully remove all of the masking fluid. Note how the effect differs between the hard line on the path, and the softer feathered lines on the foliage, where you used wetted masking fluid.

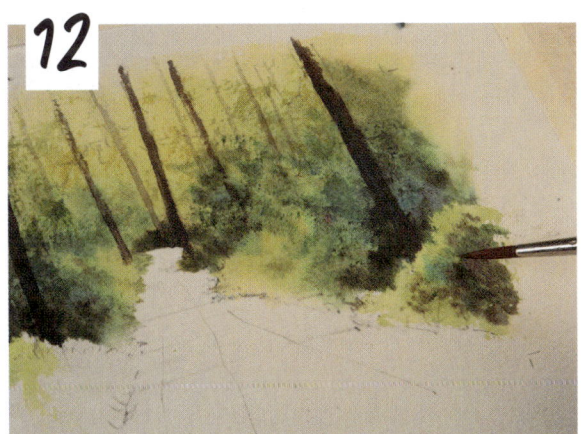

▶ Build up the woodland floor on either side of the path using a variegated wash; exactly as for the background at the top – using the same mixes and brushes. Again, leave the dilute lemon yellow visible at the top, and restrict the darker tones towards the bottom of the picture. It is important not to work up to or over the light edge you masked out at the top, or the foreground and background will merge into one area.

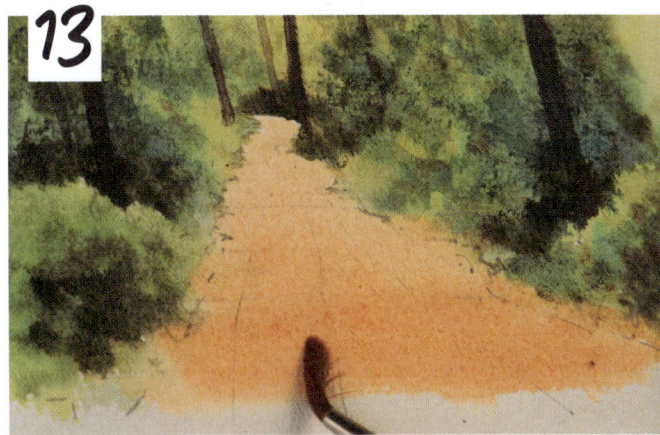

▶ Use the size 6 brush to wet the path with clean water, then drop in a thin wash of raw sienna and burnt sienna, starting from the middle of the area. Allow the paint to work upwards, but don't encourage it too much – you want the distant path to be nearly white. Add more burnt sienna to the mix for the foreground area and work down to the bottom of the painting.

TECHNIQUE: USING BODY COLOUR

Most watercolours paints are transparent or translucent, meaning that some light will still reflect from the surface of the paper beneath them, so that colours applied earlier will show through later layers, preventing you from painting light colours on top of dark ones.

Body colours are opaque. They completely cover the surface, allowing no light through, and can thus be used to add bright highlights of particular colours on top of anything beneath, even dark colours. Using body colour is a great way to suggest foliage over dark trunks and branches, as in steps 14 and 15.

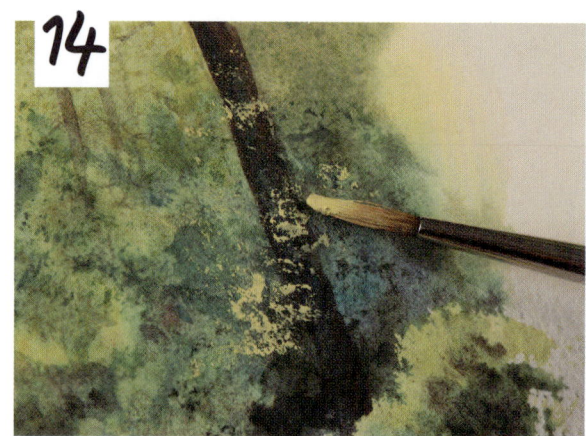

▶ To create the sunlit leaves in front of the trunks and branches of the trees, we can use opaque paint. Use the dry brush technique to apply primrose yellow as before. The opaque nature means that it will cover even the dark tones of the tree.

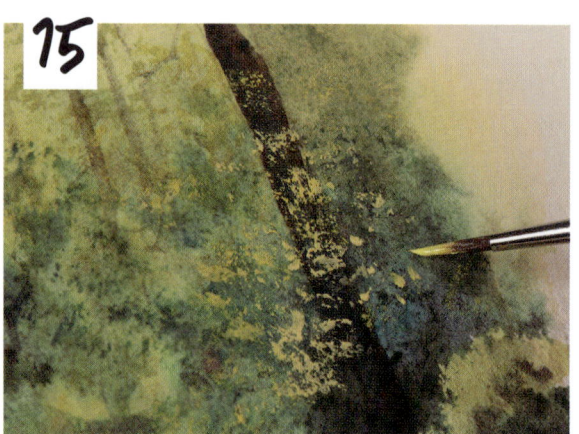

▶ Add lemon yellow touches in the same way for variety. The dark tones may show through a little, giving a semi-transparent look and stopping the body colour appearing to sit on top, which can look artificial.

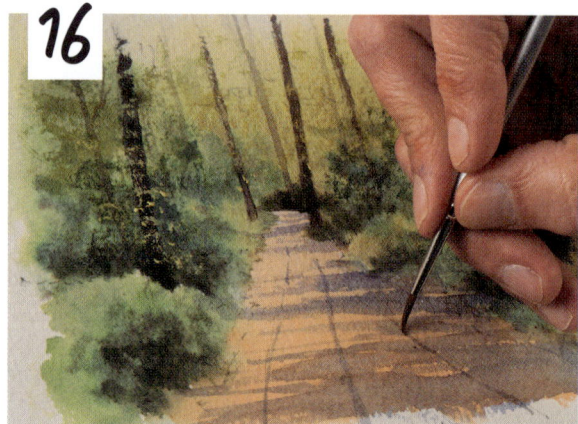

▶ Make a purple mix from cobalt blue and cobalt violet. Make it very thin – almost transparent. Use the tip of the size 2 brush to draw fine lines across the distant path as shadows. Work the shadows over the foliage at the sides, as well. The shadows should get larger as you advance towards to the front of the painting, so switch to the size 6 brush. Add a few lines to the path that lead the eye into the painting with the dilute purple mix.

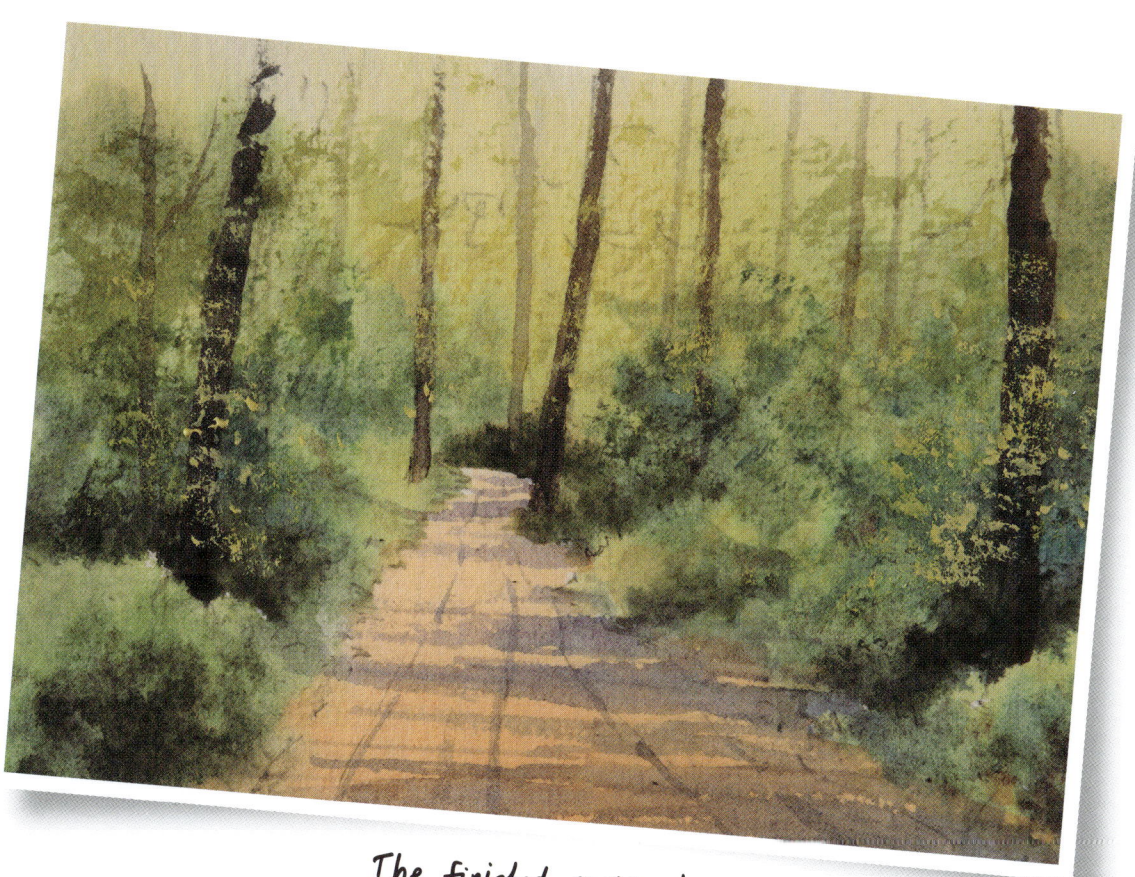

The finished postcard

Summer Trees

Sometimes it is impractical to paint a complex area wet-in-wet. You might have multiple layers to paint, or simply a lot to do. If you attempt to paint the whole area in one go, the effect when you start might be different from that at the end, as the paint has dried somewhat by the time you get to it. In order to resolve this, let the whole area dry, and then you can work on top again using techniques such as glazing and re-wetting, which are demonstrated here.

YOU WILL NEED

Paint colours: Naples yellow, cobalt violet, viridian, French ultramarine, burnt sienna, cobalt blue, rose madder, raw sienna, aureolin

Brushes: size 16 round, size 6 round, size 10 round, size 4 round, size 8 round, size 2 round

Other: putty eraser, outline drawing on page 86 (bottom)

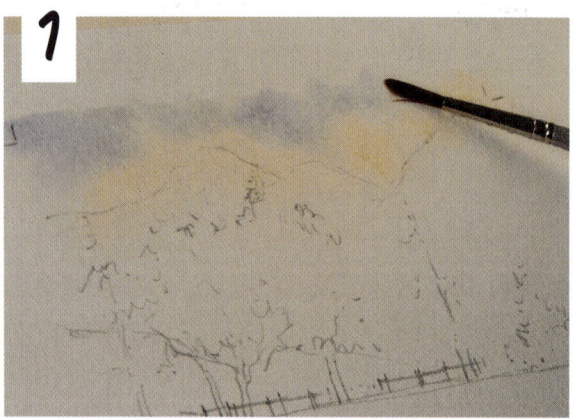

▶ Prepare a thin wash of Naples yellow and cobalt violet; a dark green wash of viridian, French ultramarine and burnt sienna; a dilute purple mix of cobalt blue and rose madder; and a thin wash of raw sienna. Use the size 16 round to wet the sky. Working from the top of the paper down and over the tops of the mountains, create a subtle variegated wash by dropping in a little of the raw sienna wash and the purple mix over the tops of the hills with the size 6 round brush.

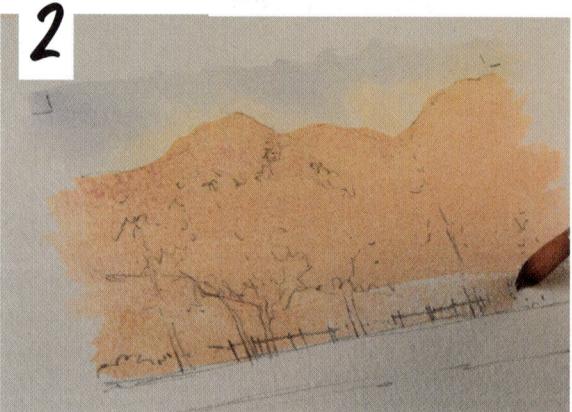

▶ Once dry, take the size 10 round to paint the background hills with the mix of Naples yellow and cobalt violet. Work down to the foreground field, leaving a level line where the background meets the line of the field. Add a touch more cobalt violet lower down.

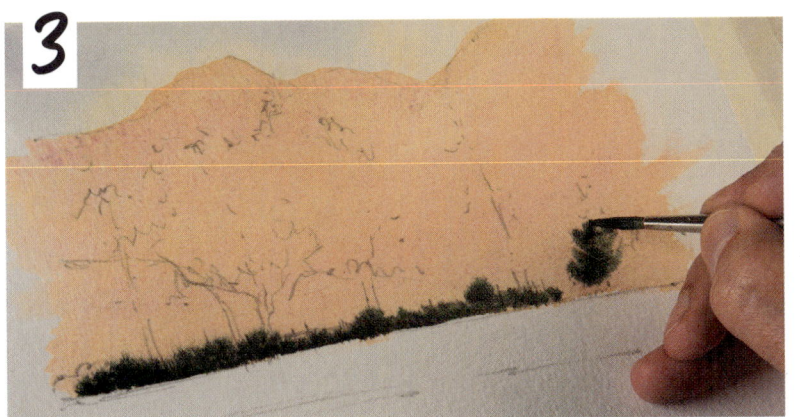

3

▶ While still wet, change to the size 4 round and paint the hedgerow at the border of the field with the dark mix. Keep the bottom of the line level, but vary the top. You can suggest small trees simply by working up into the hillside.

TECHNIQUE: GLAZING

Glazing is the process of adding a layer of colour over the top of a dry area. Because watercolour is semi-transparent, it does not obscure the colour beneath, but instead enriches it as some of the underlying colour shows through the semi-transparent glaze. Glazes are applied just like washes; just make sure the area you are working on is dry before you start.

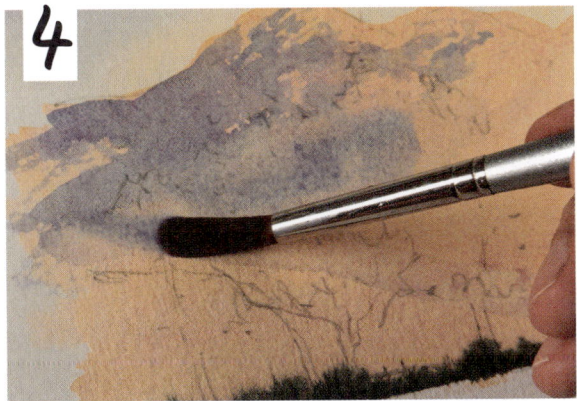

4

▶ Apart from the very crest, the hill is in shadow. Use the dilute purple mix to glaze over the top of the surface with the size 8 round. Note how the underlying colour affects the colour of the glazing paint on top. Keep in mind the direction of the light during this process.

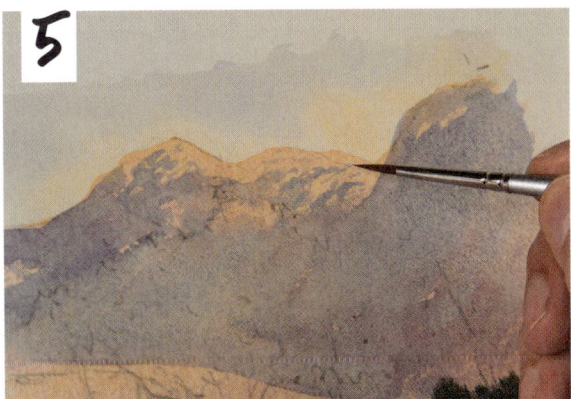

5

▶ Use the size 2 to pick out some smaller touches near the crest, creating the impression of sunlight, shadows and texture.

6

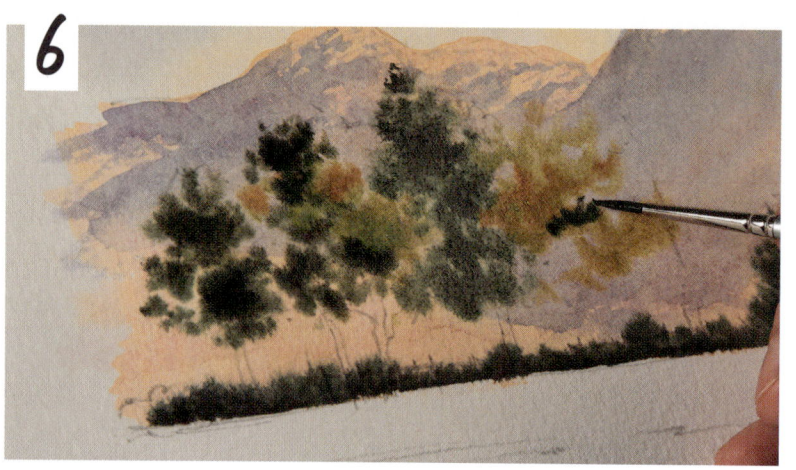

▶ Prepare plenty of the dark green mix (viridian, French ultramarine and burnt sienna) at a thick, creamy consistency, then use a clean brush to re-wet a small section, on the left-hand side, of the dry surface of the hill. Use the size 2 brush to paint in the fir trees with light touches. Vary the mix by adding touches of a light green mix of aureolin and cobalt blue; along with touches of raw sienna. Allow the area to dry, then repeat the process in an adjacent area. Continue until the whole area is complete.

TECHNIQUE: RE-WETTING

Re-wetting is a useful technique to use if you want a soft, slightly diffused finish to an area in front of a part that has already dried – as in the foliage in the step above. When re-wetting an area, work lightly to avoid disturbing the underlying colour, or the new colour will spread too far and you will end up with mud.

7

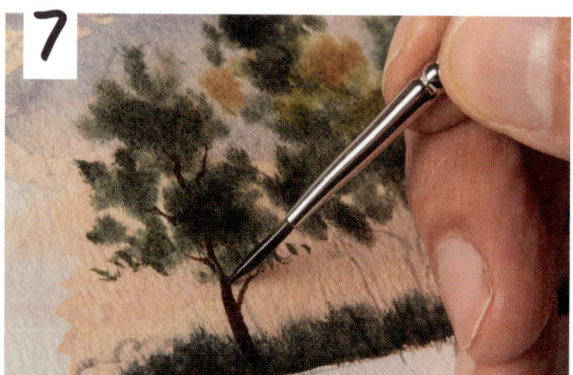

▶ Once dry, you can add trunks to connect the foliage areas to the ground using the size 2 round and a dark mix of burnt sienna and French ultramarine. Do not simply paint straight lines up and through. Instead, vary the width of the lines, and break them up inside the foliage, to suggest that the leaves are in the way.

8

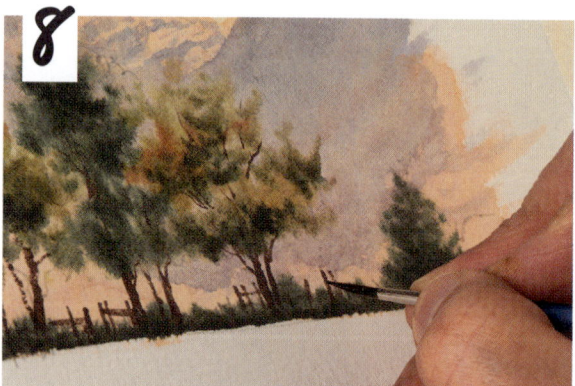

▶ Use the same mix and brush to add a few fence posts. Don't worry about being too straight and tidy; these will be more convincing if they are slightly askew.

FINISHING TOUCHES

To finish, paint the foreground field with the light green mix and the size 6 round, then add some of the dark mix wet-in-wet at the bottom to frame the area.

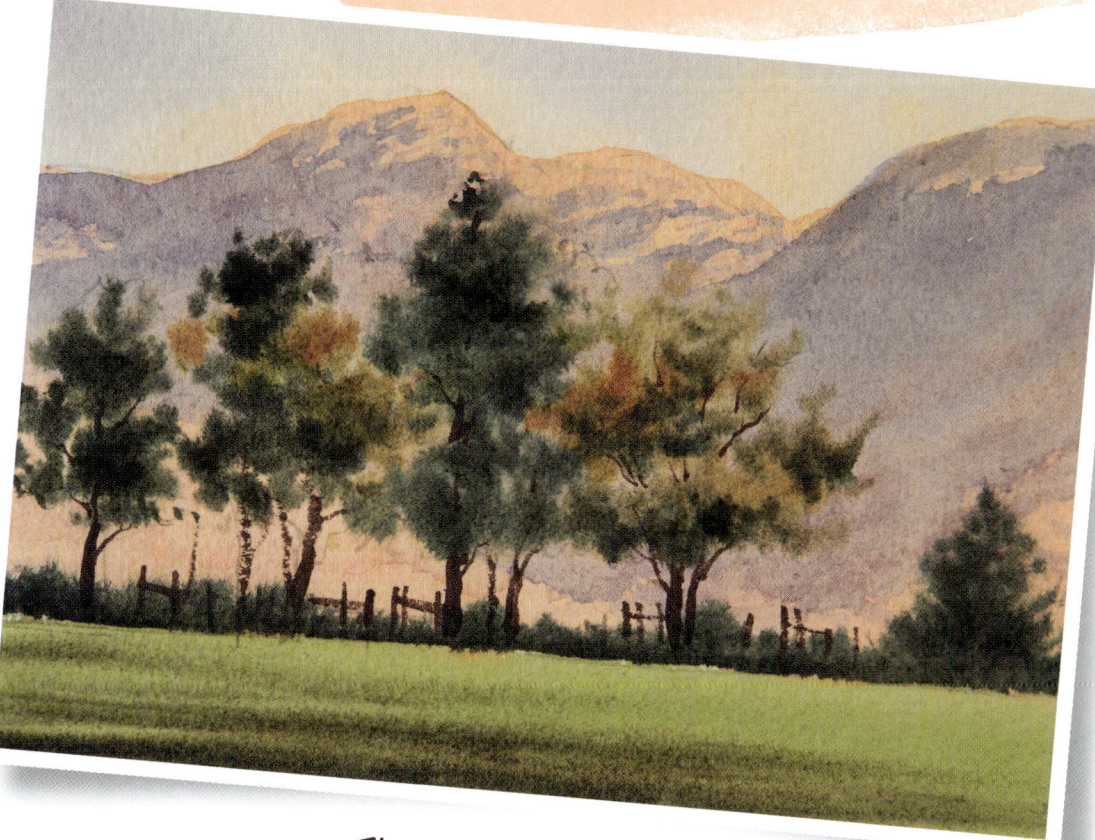

The finished postcard

Bandstand in the Park

Trees are used in this scene to draw the eye to the focal point of the park – the bandstand in the middle distance. They also act as a framing device, helping to create a relaxing, balanced image.

The foreground tree here is painted using a similar approach and techniques to the autumnal tree on pages 12–17 – once you've had a go, why not try repainting this scene in a different seasonal palette using the colours from another project?

YOU WILL NEED

Paint colours: raw sienna, burnt sienna, aureolin, cobalt blue, rose madder, viridian, French ultramarine, Naples yellow

Brushes: masking fluid brush, size 16 round, size 10 round, size 4 round

Other: masking fluid, bar of soap, outline drawing on page 87

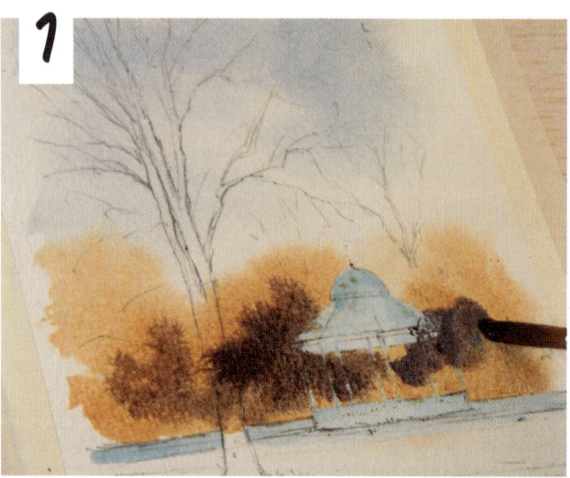

▶ Mask out the bandstand and the hedgerow. Prepare the following mixes: raw sienna and burnt sienna; aureolin and cobalt blue; a grey made from cobalt blue, rose madder and touch of burnt sienna; a dark green from viridian, French ultramarine and burnt sienna. Wet the whole of the background down to the line of the hedgerow using clean water and the size 16 brush. Be careful to wet the area within the bandstand. Change to the size 10 round and paint the sky and background wet-in-wet, adding cobalt blue near the top and the mix of raw sienna and burnt sienna near the bottom. Drop in the dark grey mix near the bottom.

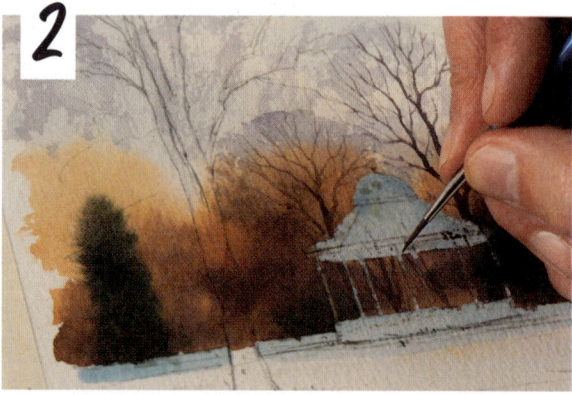

▶ Suggest small trees with dark green touches behind the hedgerow using the size 4 round. Allow to dry, then use the tip of the size 2 brush to paint in the trunk and branches of the distant tree with the grey mix. Strengthen the mix with more paint and paint the midground tree in the same way. Note how the darker tone and size make it more eye-catching than the distant tree. Add some trunks visible through the bandstand with the same brush and mix.

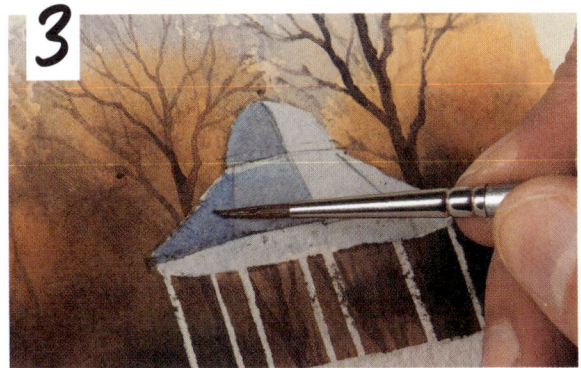

▶ Once dry, remove all of the masking fluid with a clean finger. If the masking fluid lifts off the pencil marks, re-establish them with a pencil. Paint the roof of the bandstand with the size 4 round and dilute cobalt blue. Allow to dry. The light is coming from the right-hand side, so add the shading on the left-hand side of the roof. Lay in a wash of cobalt blue over the areas, then touch in the grey mix wet-in-wet near the bottom of each panel in shade. You can make the leftmost areas still darker with a third layer, but do make sure the previous layer is dry first.

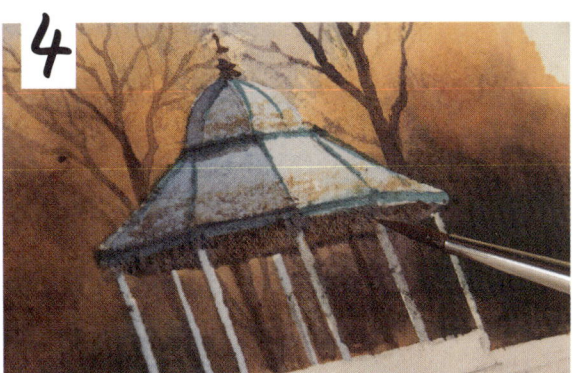

▶ Use the tip of the size 2 brush to touch a little of the raw sienna and burnt sienna mix, and the brown mix (cobalt blue, rose madder and burnt sienna) onto the bandstand to make it appear lightly weathered. Mix viridian with cobalt blue and paint in the steelwork with this blue-green, then shade it with a glaze of the grey mix. Paint the underside of the roof with the same grey mix, touching in some of the raw sienna and burnt sienna mix for interest. Tint the uprights with cobalt blue. Once dry, use the tip of the size 2 brush to suggest a few posts at the back in shadow, using the brown mix.

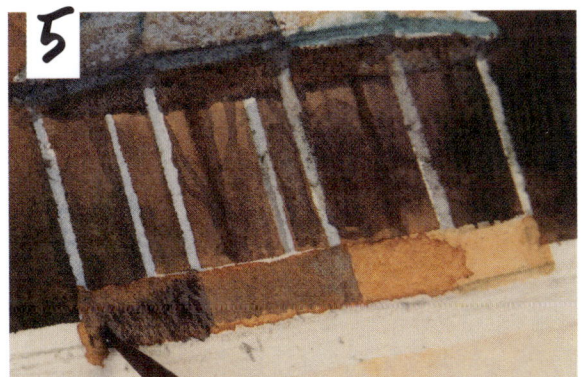

▶ Paint the stonework pedestal on which the bandstand is built using raw sienna and burnt sienna, applying the paint with the size 4 brush. Allow it to dry, then glaze the left-hand side with the grey mix (cobalt blue, rose madder and a touch of burnt sienna). Repeat to build up a gradual sense of shadow and suggest the angular shape of the base.

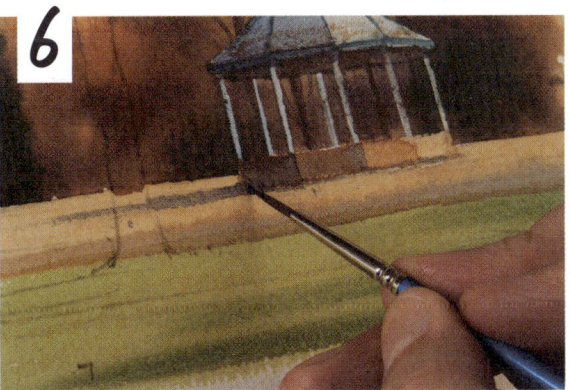

▶ Paint in the path using raw sienna and burnt sienna, adding a shadow using the grey mix. Paint the grass using the aureolin and cobalt blue mix. Add shadows wet-in-wet on the grass with the dark green mix (viridian, French ultramarine and burnt sienna), and behind the bandstand with the grey mix.

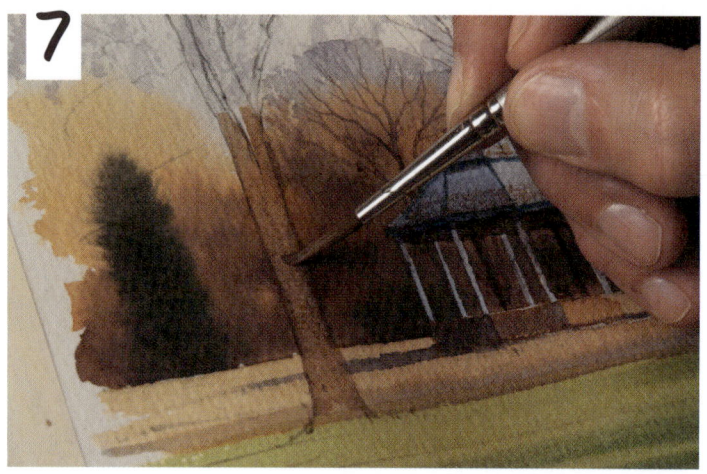

▶ Make three mixes: a light tone of Naples yellow and burnt sienna, a mid-grey mix of cobalt blue, rose madder and burnt sienna, and a dark brown mix of burnt sienna and French ultramarine. Using the size 4 brush, paint the trunk of the tree with the light-toned mix and allow to dry.

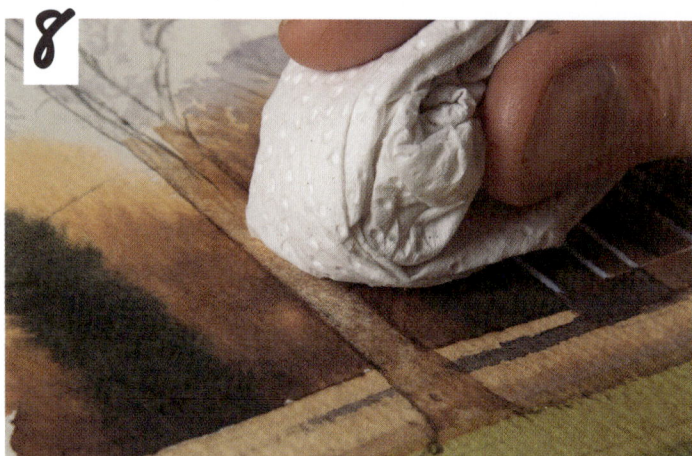

▶ Gently agitate the paint on the large foreground tree with a damp brush, then press a clean piece of kitchen paper onto the area. This will lift away a little of the wet paint to create a soft highlight.

TECHNIQUE: LIFTING OUT

This technique allows you to create highlights over dry paint. You can also lift out areas from first washes, drawing up excess paint and leaving a paler area.

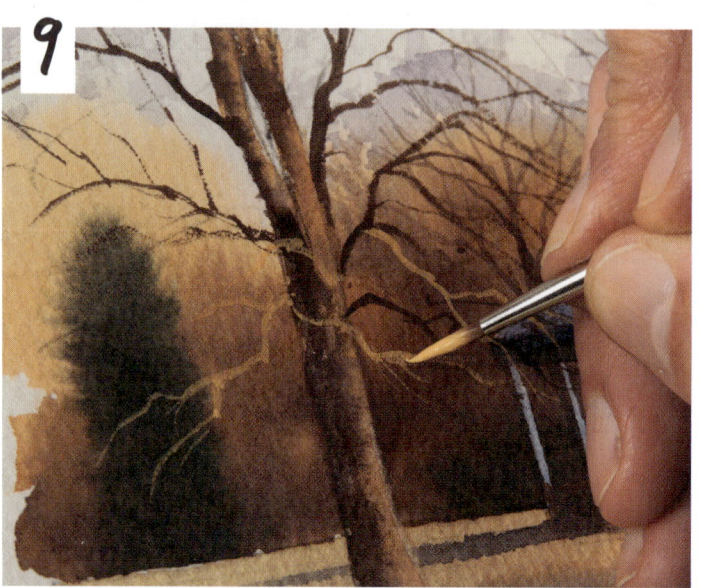

▶ Detail the foreground tree with touches of the mid-grey mix followed by the dark mix wet-in-wet, avoiding the right-hand side. Build up the main branches in the same way. Paying attention to how the branches arc away and downwards under their own weight, use the dark mix to paint finer branches, and pure Naples yellow for those in direct sunlight, using the same brush and technique. These are particularly effective in front of the darker areas of background.

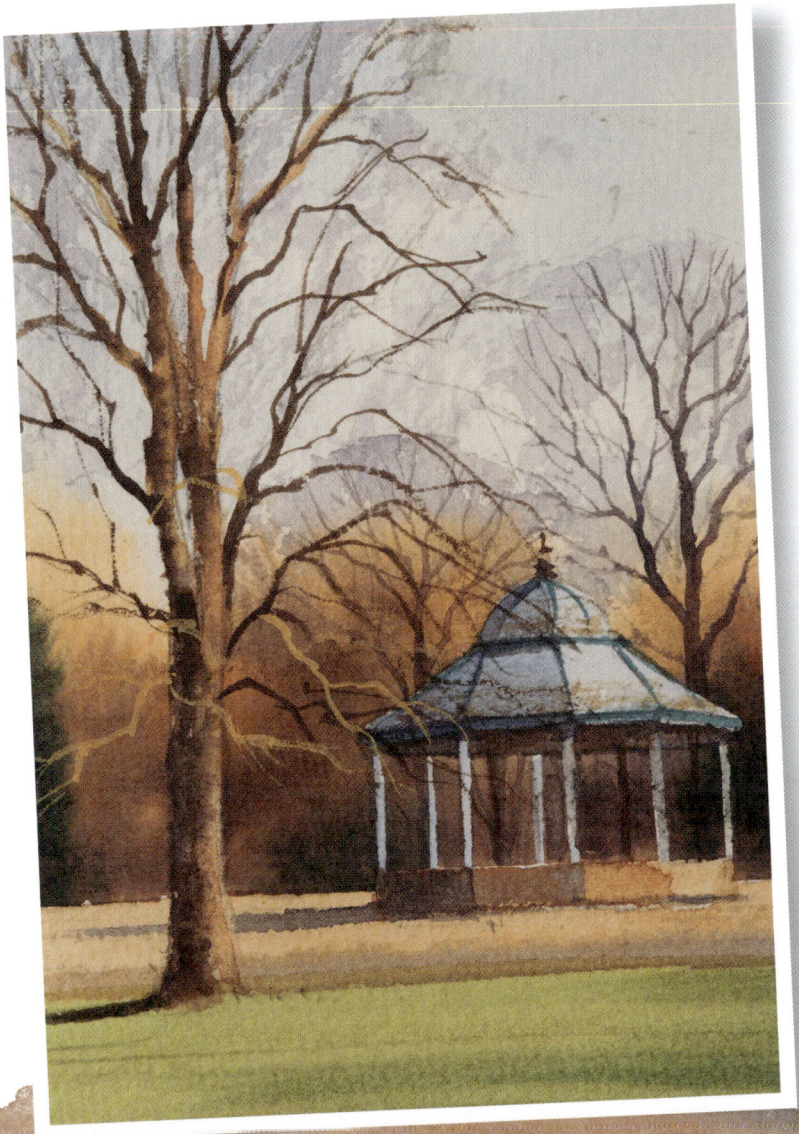

FINISHING TOUCHES

To finish, soften the base of the tree with clean water and dark brown, then paint the shadow cast by the tree using the size 2 brush and the dark green mix (viridian, French ultramarine and burnt sienna).

Bluebell Wood

This project looks again at feathered masking, in which masking fluid is applied to a wet surface. This causes it to flow a little and allows you to avoid the hard edges typically associated with masking fluid.

Note that, despite the name, bluebells are commonly more violet than blue, so make sure to include a fair amount of the cobalt violet when preparing the paint mix for these beautiful flowers.

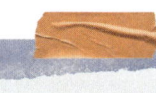

YOU WILL NEED

Paint colours: primrose yellow, aureolin, cobalt blue, viridian, French ultramarine, burnt sienna, cobalt violet, white gouache

Brushes: size 10 round, masking fluid brush, size 6 round, size 4 round

Other: masking fluid, bar of soap, outline drawing on page 88 (top)

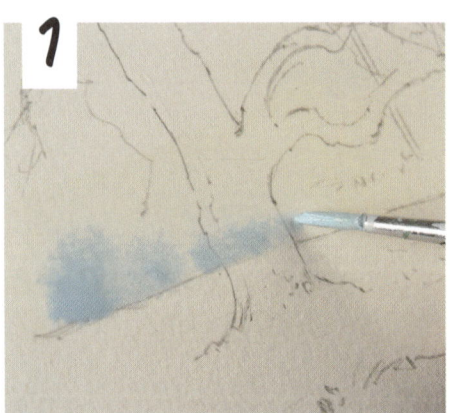

▶ Wet the paper just above the bottom third of the painting, following the line on the outline drawing, using clean water and the size 10 round brush. Tip your board at an angle to prevent it running too far upwards, then add masking fluid above the line. This will bloom upwards to create soft foliage later. Allow to dry.

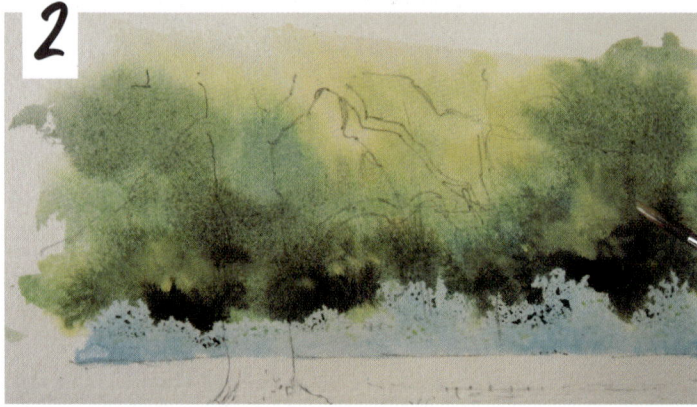

▶ Prepare the following mixes: primrose yellow at a very thin consistency; a bright green mix of aureolin and cobalt blue; a blue-green mix of viridian and cobalt blue; and a dark green mix of viridian, French ultramarine and burnt sienna. Wet the whole background down to the masking fluid, then create a variegated wash using the size 10 round and primrose yellow; dropping in bright green and then blue green wet-in-wet. Switch to the size 6 brush and drop in areas of the dark green mix wet-in-wet, concentrating it immediately above the masking fluid.

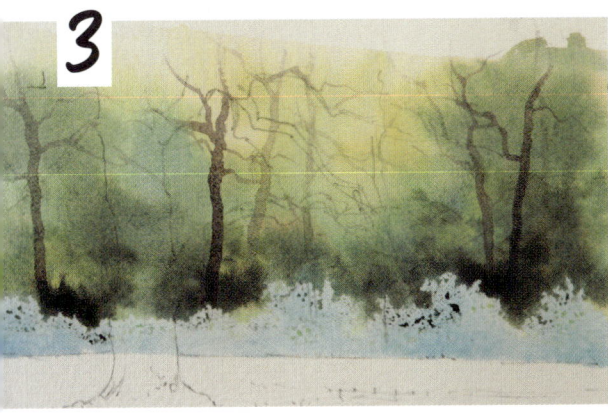

▶ Pick up some thick primrose yellow from the palette well, then add it in at the top of the dark green areas. This will help blend the colours in the background together. Once dry, create a grey mix of cobalt blue, cobalt violet and burnt sienna and use the size 2 round brush to paint the background trees. Vary the consistency of the mix to create different tones.

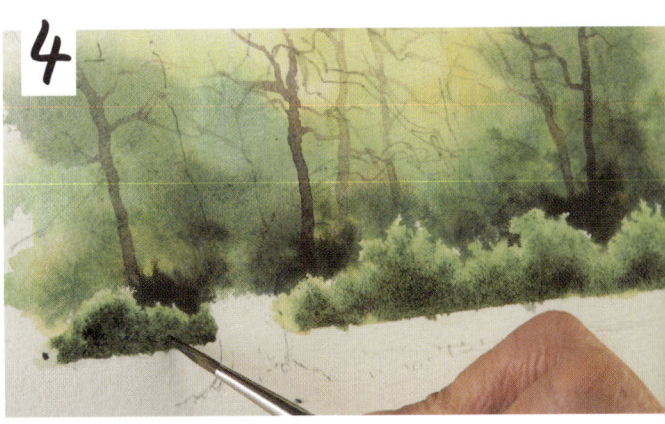

▶ Once dry, remove the masking fluid with a clean finger to reveal a soft edge. Apply dilute primrose yellow to the revealed foliage shapes using a size 6 round brush, stopping at the edge of the big tree. Drop in the bright green, then the blue-green, then the dark green mixes wet-in-wet, covering increasingly less of the area and not allowing it to blot out the light at the top edges of the bushes. You may find it easier to swap to the size 4 for the dark green additions, as these cover very little of the area.

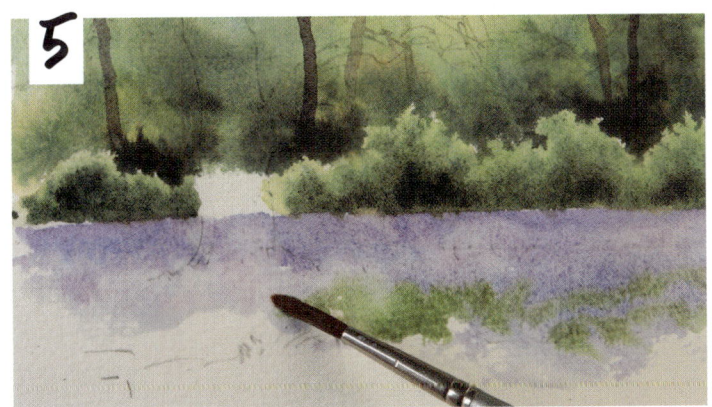

▶ Make a bluebell mix from cobalt blue and cobalt violet. Using a size 6 brush, paint the foreground forest floor with the bluebell mix, working right the way across the big tree. Add some clean water here and there to keep the colours soft. You want to create the impression of a mass of bluebells in this area, not individual flowers. Add the bright green and blue-green mixes wet-in-wet at the bottom of the area.

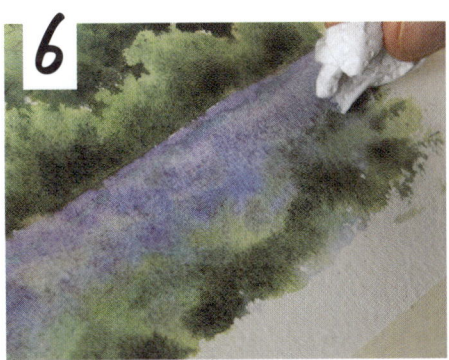

▶ Change to the size 4 round brush and add in stronger touches of the bluebell mix to enrich the colour near the foreground. Use the side of the size 4 brush to darken the foreground with the dark green mix. Lift out a few subtle areas from the bluebells using some clean kitchen paper.

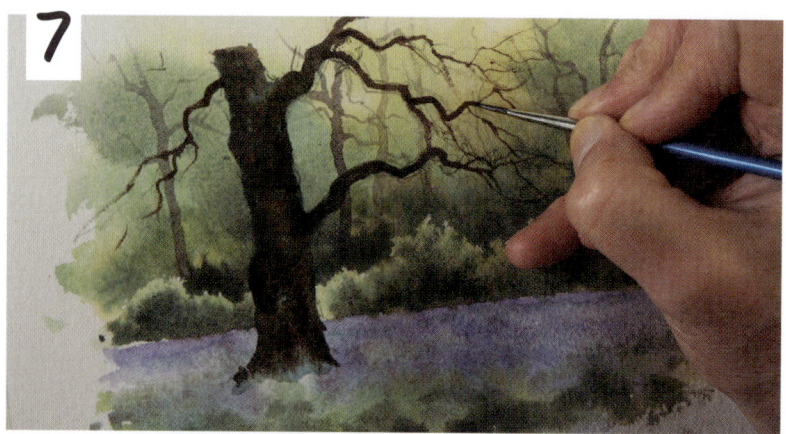

▶ Once dry, drop in a mix of viridian and cobalt blue on the trunk of the big tree, then add a rich dark brown mix of French ultramarine and burnt sienna wet-in-wet. Add some branches with the same dark mix and the tip of the size 2 round brush.

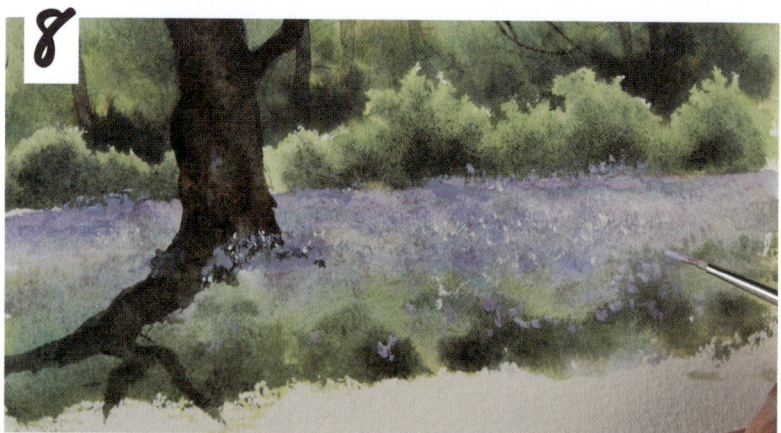

▶ Extend the dark green to the lower left to create a cast shadow. Brush some of the dark mix from the tree itself into the shadow to show that shadows are darkest nearest the object casting them. Mix cobalt blue and cobalt violet into white gouache to make an opaque bluebell colour. Apply this mix over the bluebells and the base of the tree with the size 2 round and the dry brush technique.

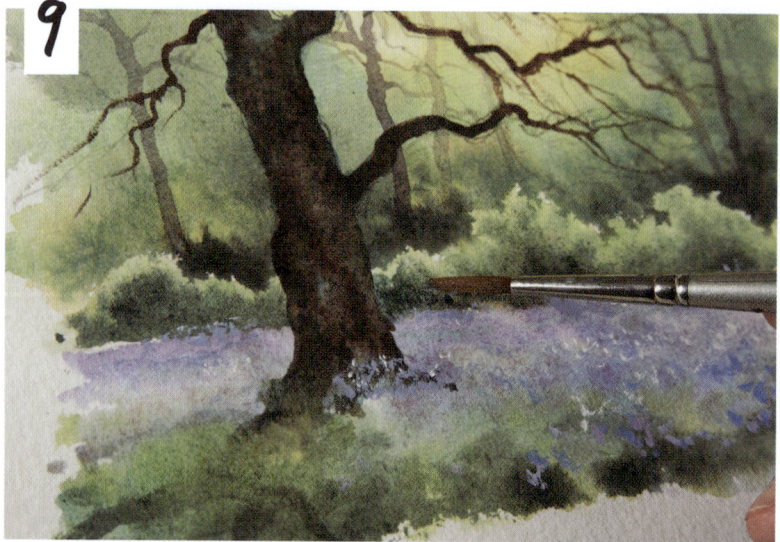

▶ Wet the shadow of the tree with a clean damp brush, then add a little dilute lemon yellow to soften it into the undergrowth. Strengthen the dark green in the bushes next to the tree for added contrast.

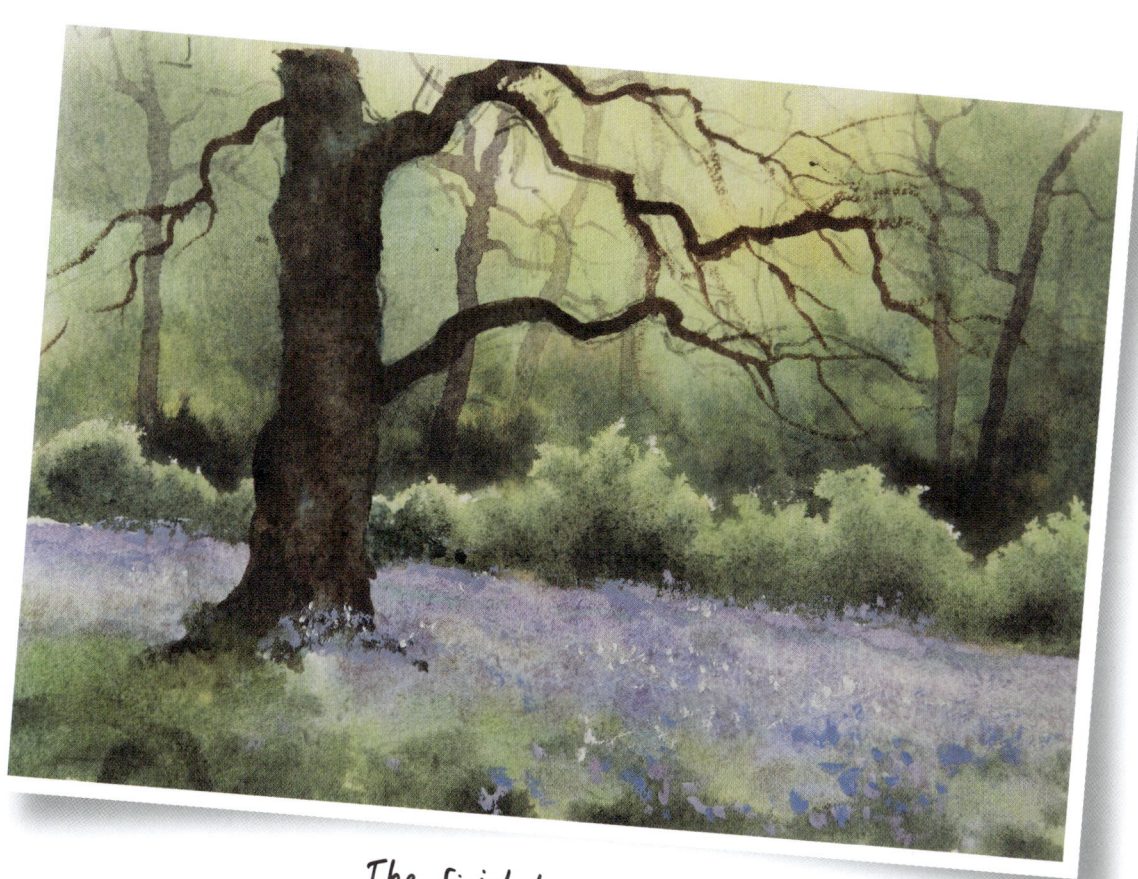

The finished postcard

Farmhouse

There is no need to rush when painting this charming scene, particularly near the start. If you go in too quickly, the variegated wash will bleed too far, or the colours merge too much. The surface needs simply to be wet enough for the paint to flow a little. If you do find the paint running too far upwards into the sky, prop your board up at a slight angle until the surface dries a little.

This project also introduces negative painting, a technique that involves painting the area around an object, rather than the object itself. This is a good way to ensure clean lines in your work.

YOU WILL NEED

Paint colours: aureolin, burnt sienna, cobalt blue, viridian, French ultramarine, burnt sienna, rose madder, lemon yellow

Brushes: masking fluid brush, size 16 brush, size 10 brush, size 2 brush, size 6 brush

Other: masking fluid, bar of soap, outline drawing on page 88 (bottom)

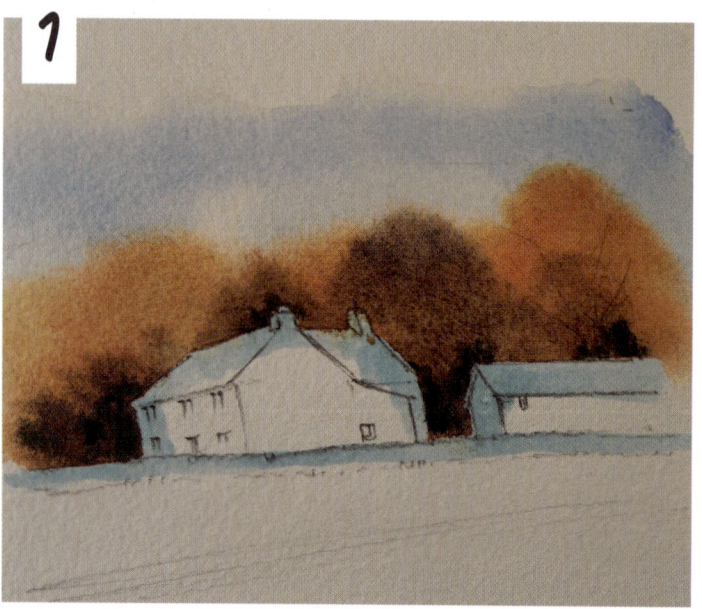

▶ Mask the two buildings and the wall in front of them and allow them to dry. Prepare the following mixes: an orange made from aureolin and burnt sienna at a fairly thick consistency, a little like full cream milk; a thin wash of cobalt blue; a brown made from burnt sienna and cobalt blue; and a green from viridian, French ultramarine and burnt sienna. Use the size 16 round to wet the sky with clean water, working around but not over the buildings. Change to the size 10 brush and paint the sky with the thin cobalt blue. While wet, float in the orange, brown and green mixes around the trees, concentrating the darker colours nearer the buildings. Allow to dry.

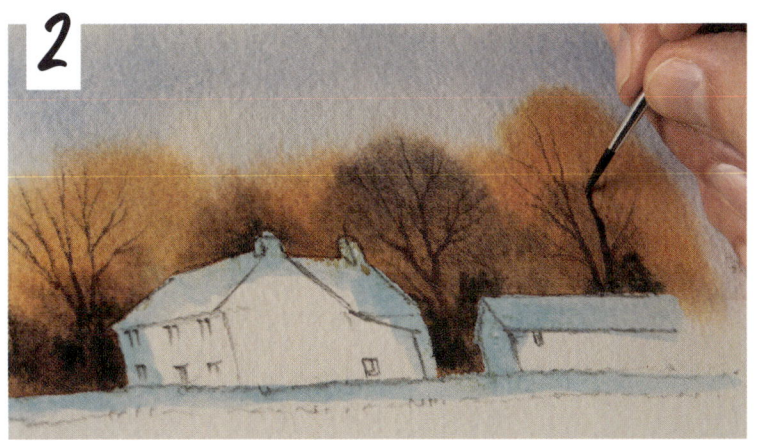

2

▶ Paint in the trunks and main branches using the brown mix (burnt sienna and cobalt blue), applying the paint with the tip of the size 2 brush. As always, taper the branches outwards, but don't work right to the edge of the coloured foliage area.

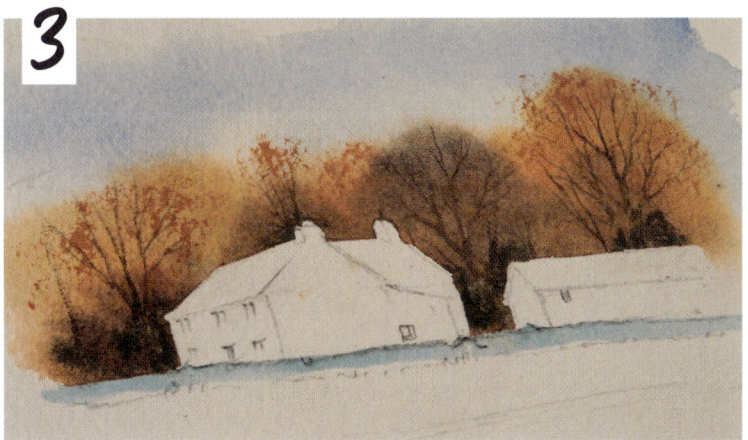

3

▶ Make a thick opaque orange mix from lemon yellow and burnt sienna. Use the dry brush technique to add some detail to the foliage over the main branches. Allow to dry, then gently remove the masking fluid from the buildings only – leave it in place on the wall. If you accidentally rub a little of the wall masking away, you can reapply the masking fluid if you wish, or just work carefully around the area.

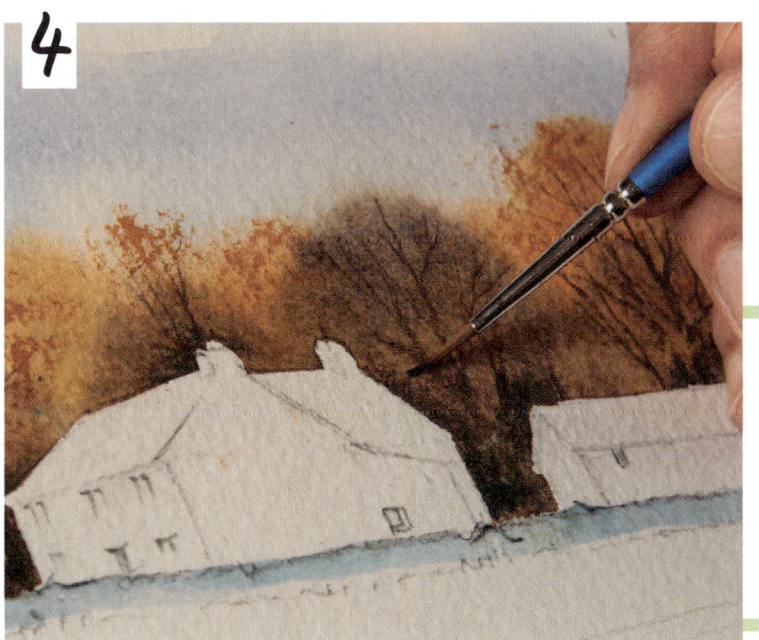

4

▶ When you remove the masking fluid, you may find the is line not quite straight, or doesn't quite reach the area that you wanted reserved. In these cases, use a fine brush to paint the background colour up to the edge, then soften it away into the background.

TECHNIQUE: NEGATIVE PAINTING

Step 4 is an example of negative painting. Instead of painting the shape itself, you paint the area up to and around it, to leave a space in the correct shape.

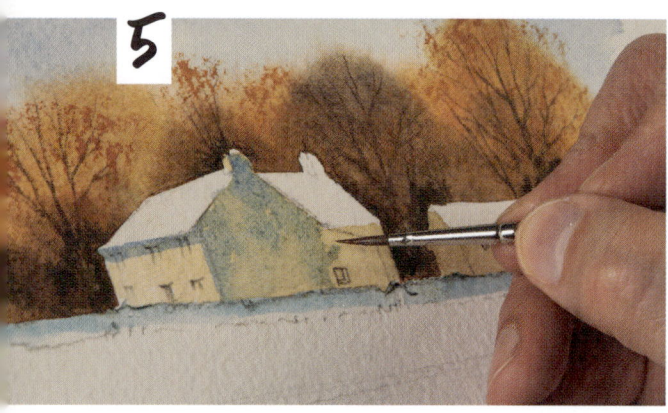

▶ Use a very dilute mix of aureolin and burnt sienna to paint in the farmhouse on the left-hand side with the size 6 brush. Once this has dried, add more burnt sienna for a slightly darker variation and paint in the barn on the right-hand side. Leave the roofs clean, but paint right over the windows. Add some shadow to the buildings with a glaze of dilute cobalt blue. Pay attention to the light source (in this case, the light is coming from the top left) to help you work out where to place the shadows.

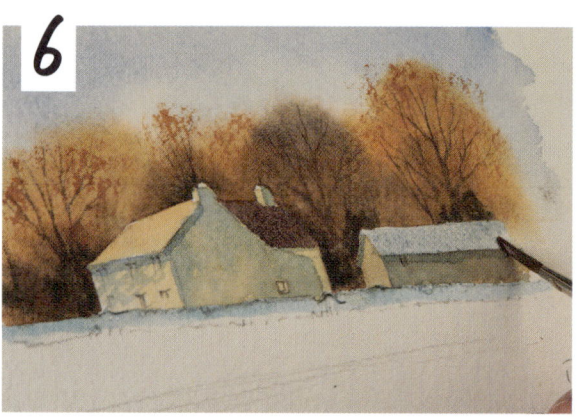

▶ Change to the size 6 round. Add a touch of rose madder to burnt sienna and cobalt blue to make a deep, warm brown. Use this to paint the farmhouse roof in shadow, then paint the barn roof with dilute cobalt blue.

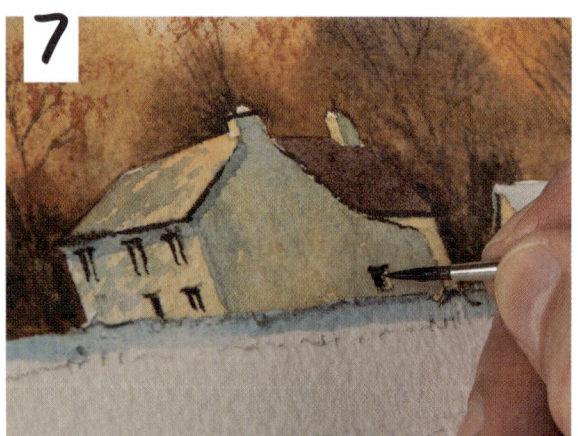

▶ Add texture to the farmhouse roof with the same loose touches of dilute cobalt blue. Add more detail to the buildings with the very dark mix (French ultramarine and burnt sienna), picking out the edges of the roofs, deep shadows and windows with the very tip of the size 2 round.

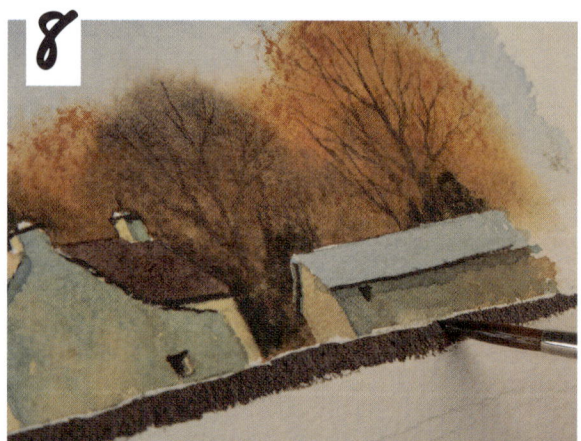

▶ Use the dry brush technique to add foliage in front of the farmhouse with the opaque orange mix, then rub away the remaining masking fluid and paint the wall using the brown mix (burnt sienna and cobalt blue), leaving a white gap at the top.

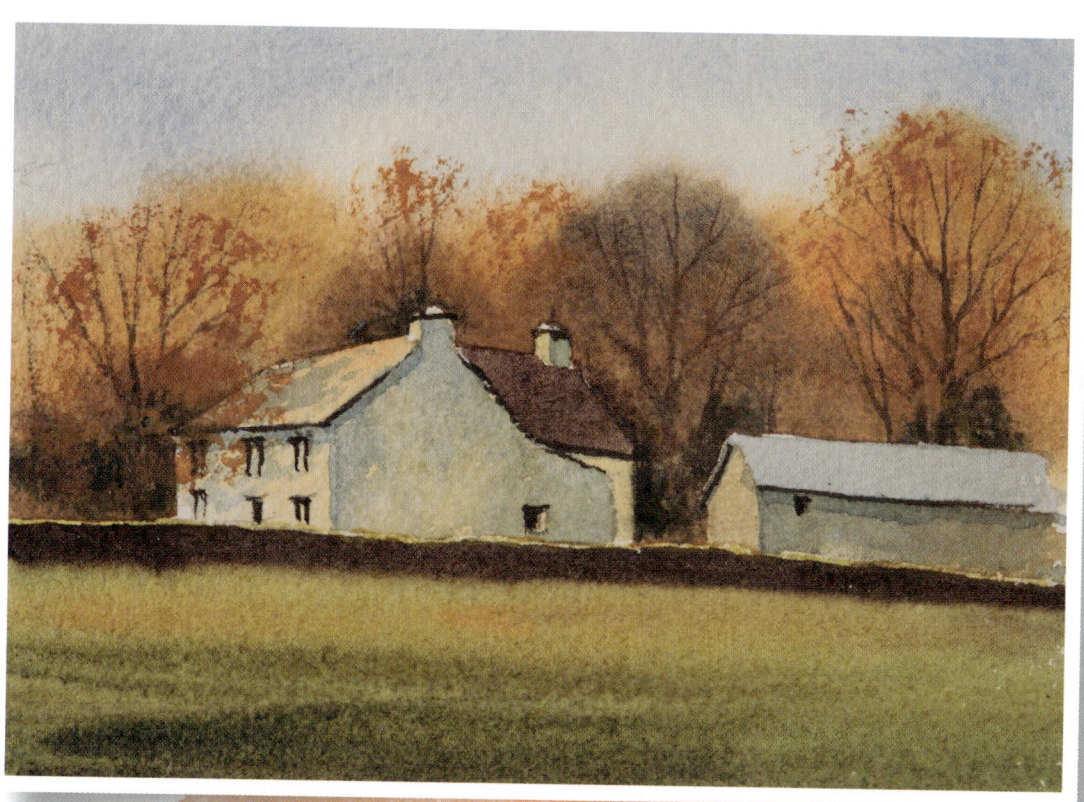

FINISHING TOUCHES

To finish, add the bright green mix into the foreground field while the wall is still wet so that the two areas blend. Add aureolin, burnt sienna and the dark green mix to the field wet-in-wet for an autumnal feel, and paint the white gap at the top of the hedge using aureolin to prevent it being too stark.

City Trees

This more complex postcard painting does not introduce any new techniques, but instead is an opportunity for you to consolidate what you have learned so far. It is a great example of what you can achieve with watercolour. The tree here is the focus, but the hard lines and complex silhouette of the building behind provide an interesting counterpoint to the soft foliage.

Before you begin, prepare a well of dilute cobalt blue, then mix a grey from cobalt blue, rose madder and a little burnt sienna, plus a warm orange mix of cadmium yellow and burnt sienna.

YOU WILL NEED

Paint colours: cobalt blue, rose madder, burnt sienna, cadmium yellow, French ultramarine, lemon yellow

Brushes: size 10 round, size 6 round, size 4 round, size 2 round

Other: outline drawing on page 89

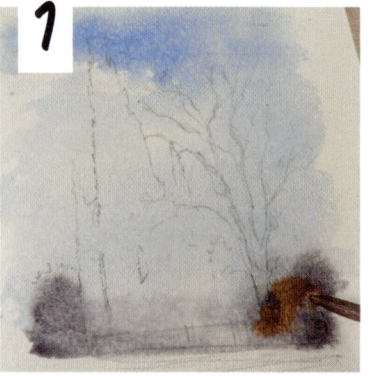

▶ Use a size 10 to wet the sky area (including the tree and building). Leave a few streaks of dry paper at the top, and a gap behind the building. Starting from the top of the paper, drop in the dilute cobalt blue over the sky area, steering clear of the gap and adding pure water towards the bottom. Drop in the grey mix to suggest background buildings, then add touches of the warm orange mix wet-in-wet.

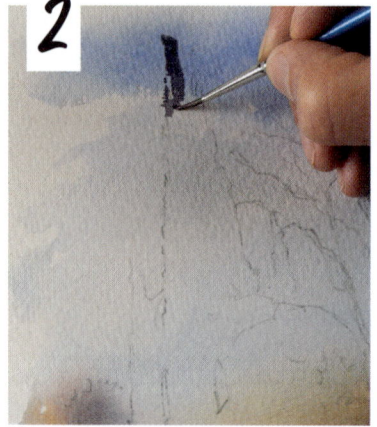

▶ While the painting dries, prepare a thicker version of the grey mix. Starting with the dilute grey mix, paint in the top of the main building using the size 2 round. Work wet on dry, with close reference to the original image. Treat the shape as a silhouette. This will simplify things and prevent the building becoming overly complex.

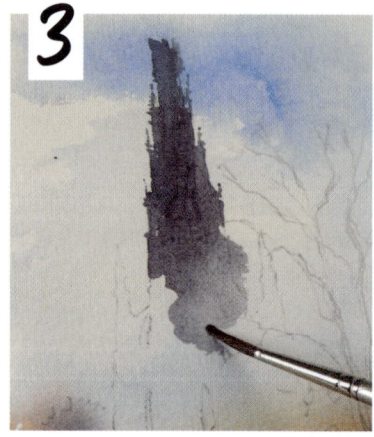

▶ Change to the size 4 as you work down the building to allow you to work fairly rapidly – if you work too slowly, you will end up with a patchy result. Add some water near the tree, to dilute the grey behind the foliage.

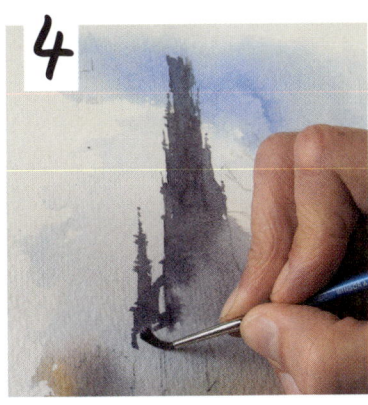

▶ Introduce the stronger, darker grey mix towards the bottom of the building, and use the dilute, thin mix for areas behind the tree. Pay attention to the gaps near the bottom, but remember you are aiming to suggest the general sense of the building's shape, not for exacting architectural accuracy.

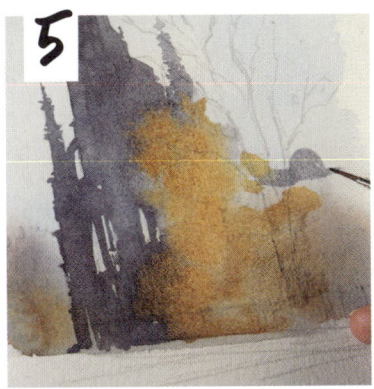

▶ Introduce the warm orange mix wet-in-wet around the building using the size 6 round brush, then swap to the size 2 round brush to develop the dome on the right with the grey mix. This will help to suggest the border of the tree.

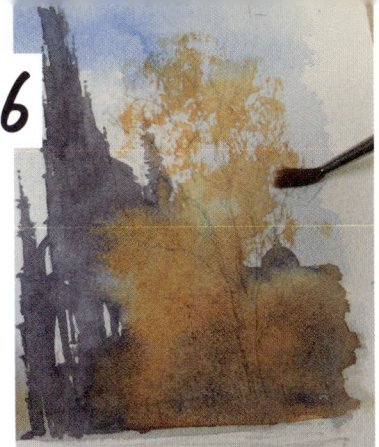

▶ Swap back to the size 6 round brush and develop the foliage with more of the warm orange mix, working the paint into the wet paint of the bottom of the dome. Use the dry brush technique above the dome to create the impression of texture.

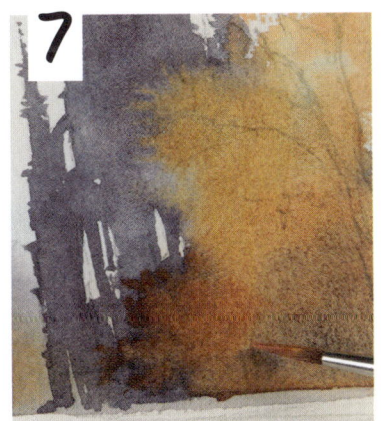

▶ Warm the mix with burnt sienna and vary the foliage.

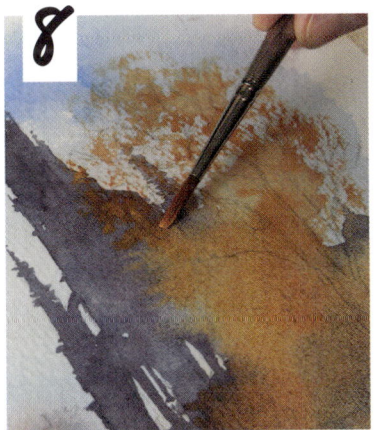

▶ Pick out a few loose leaves in front of the building with some neat cadmium yellow added wet-in-wet to the dry-brushed foliage.

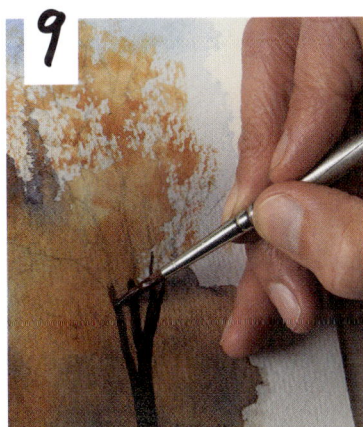

▶ Make a dark brown from burnt sienna and French ultramarine and paint in the trunk of the tree with the size 4 round.

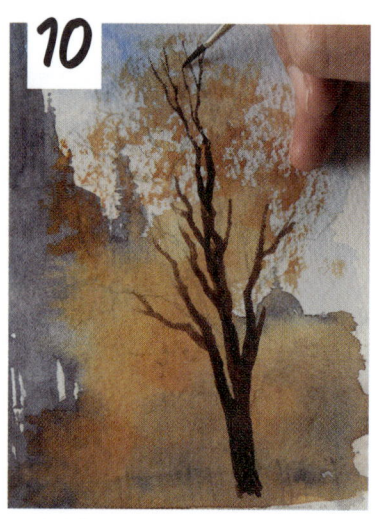

10

▶ Work the tree upwards from the base, splitting it into the main branches. Change to the size 2 round brush for the finer branches, working up to, but not beyond, the edge of the foliage.

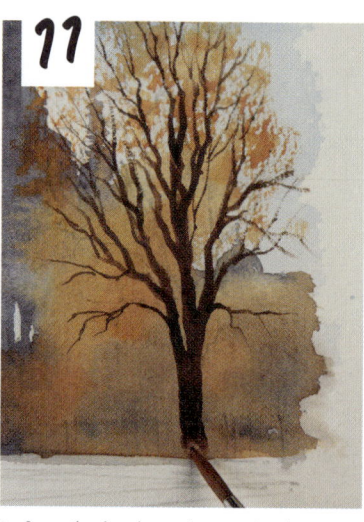

11

▶ Once the fine branches are in place, soften the base of the tree into the ground with clean water.

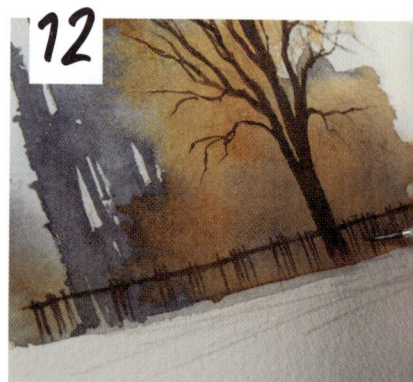

12

▶ Paint the fence with the size 2 round and the same dark brown mix, making the line for the top rail quickly to help you get a straight line. As you put in the posts, paint downwards from the railing. Work in clusters rather than simply from left to right: a few gaps in it suggest plants growing through the fence.

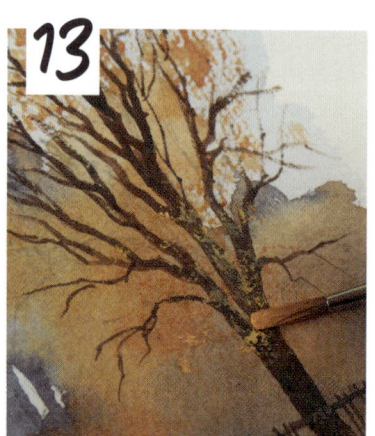

13

▶ Use the size 4 brush and the dry brush technique to add pure cadmium yellow highlights across the tree. Repeat the process with a mix of lemon yellow and burnt sienna.

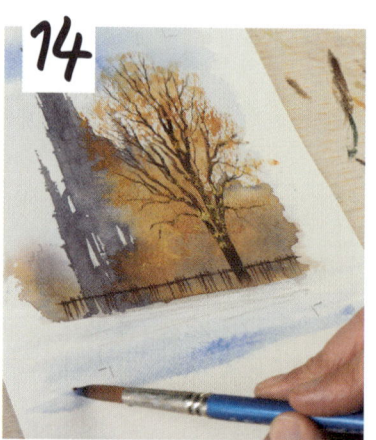

14

▶ Wet the road with clean water, then drop in dilute cobalt blue mix with the size 10 round. Using some of the sky colour in the foreground helps to unify the image.

15

▶ Once dry, suggest the edge of the kerb with the size 2 round and the stronger grey mix. Mix cobalt blue and rose madder for a shadow mix and bring the colour across the road with quick horizontal strokes, using the tip of the size 4 round brush.

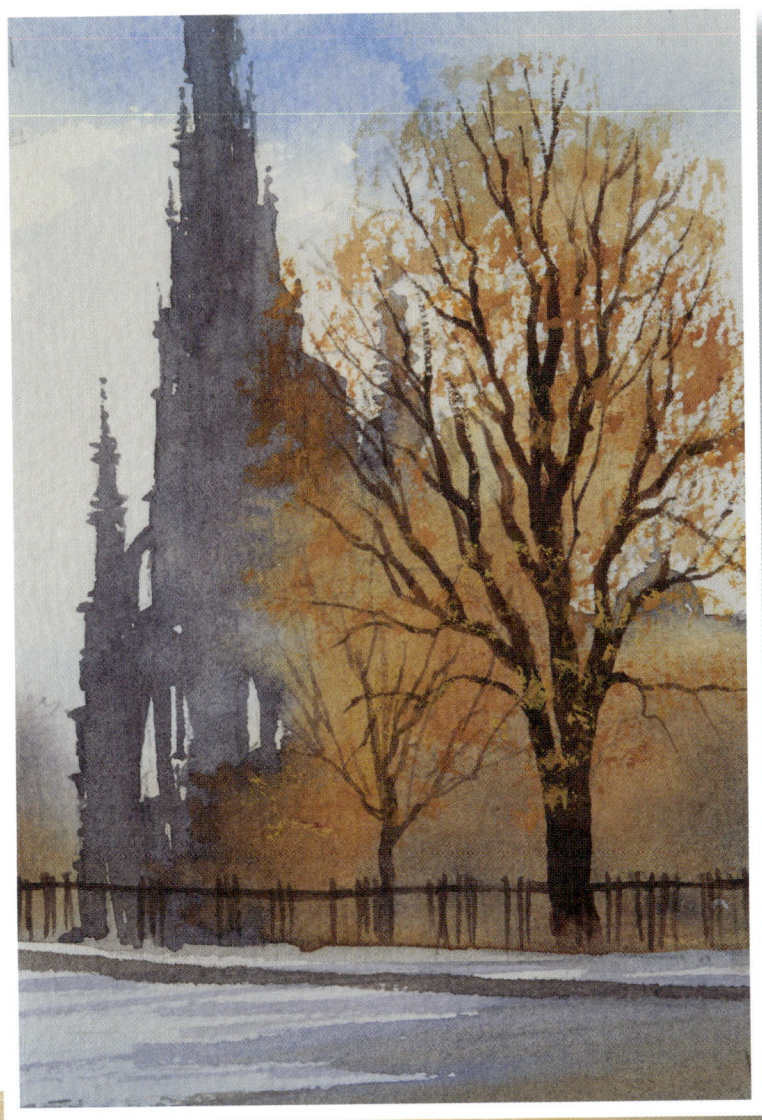

FINISHING TOUCHES

To finish, use the more dilute grey mix to add a distant tree near the centre of the painting with the size 2 round brush. This will lead the eye more towards the centre of the image.

Weeping Willow

Willows are attractive and distinctive riverside trees which can be painted with a few simple techniques. Since they are most commonly found near riverbanks, this postcard painting also includes a simple river, to introduce you to painting water.

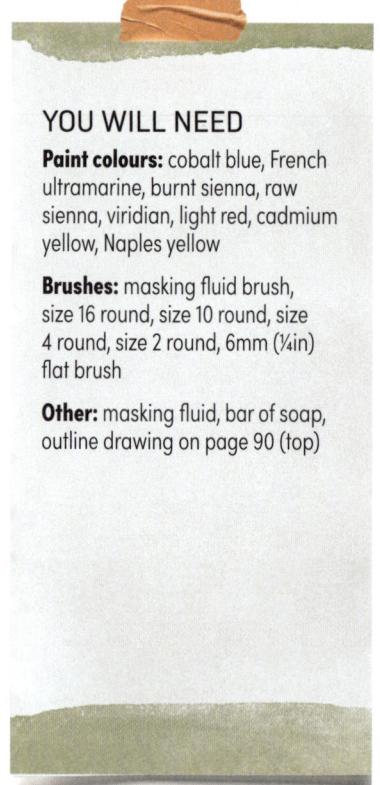

YOU WILL NEED

Paint colours: cobalt blue, French ultramarine, burnt sienna, raw sienna, viridian, light red, cadmium yellow, Naples yellow

Brushes: masking fluid brush, size 16 round, size 10 round, size 4 round, size 2 round, 6mm (¼in) flat brush

Other: masking fluid, bar of soap, outline drawing on page 90 (top)

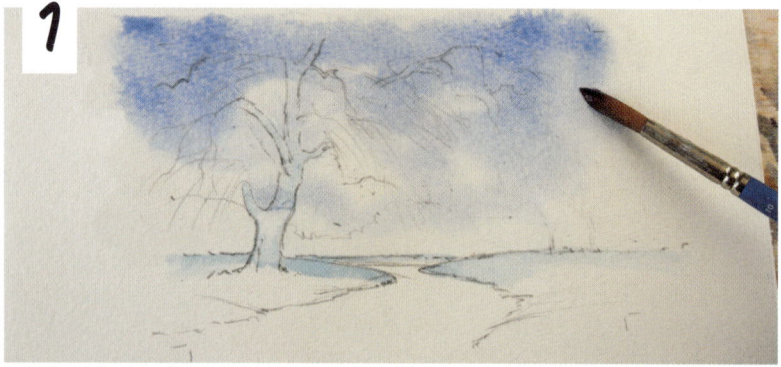

▶ Use masking fluid to mask the distant bank, the two middle distant riverbanks, and the trunk of the willow. Use a size 16 round brush to wet the background down to the ground level, then change to a size 10 and drop in a sky blue mix of cobalt blue and French ultramarine, making the colour stronger towards the top and lighter towards the horizon.

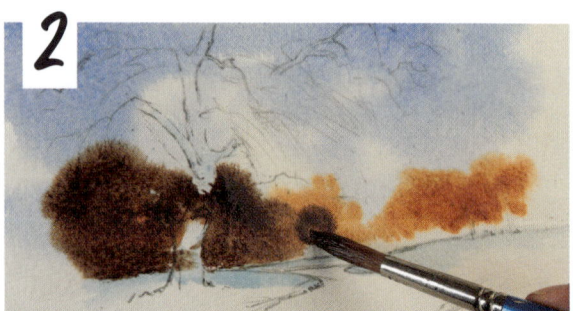

▶ Drop in a warm orange mix of raw sienna and burnt sienna wet-in-wet with the size 4 round to suggest distant trees. Change to a thick nut-brown mix of burnt sienna and cobalt blue, and apply it with the size 10 round brush all along the horizon, over and around the orange area.

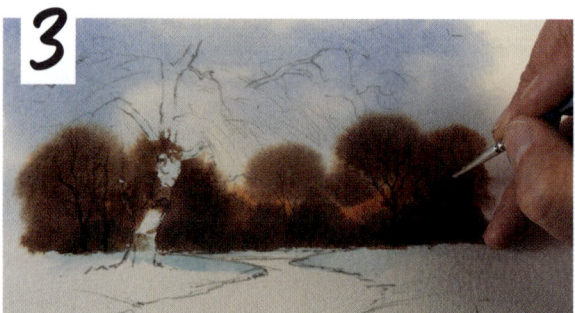

▶ Strengthen the colour near the ground by adding more paint to the mix and touching it in wet-in-wet. Allow the paint to dry. Use a size 2 round brush to draw out the trunks and branches of the background trees with the nut-brown mix.

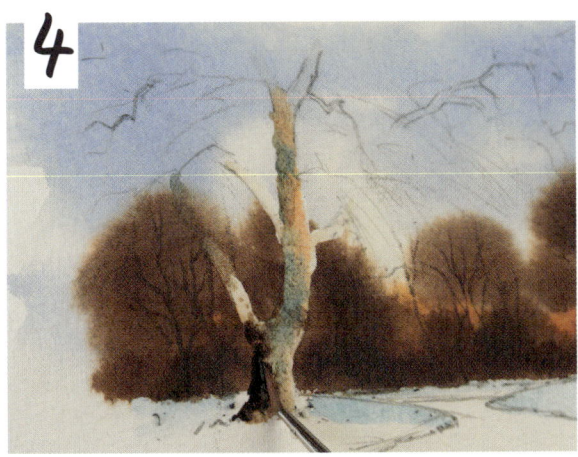

4

▶ Remove the masking fluid from the tree with a clean finger. Prepare the following mixes: a blue-green of cobalt blue and viridian; a warm mix of light red and raw sienna; and a dark mix of burnt sienna and French ultramarine. Wet the tree with clean water using a size 4 round. Drop in the warm mix, then add the blue-green mix wet-in-wet. Add dark brown on the left of the tree with the size 2 round brush.

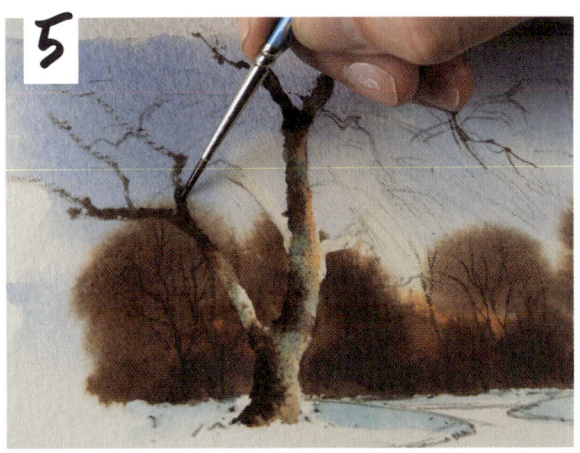

5

▶ Use the same nut-brown mix and size 2 brush to add the main branches. Perhaps contrary to expectations, these generally point upwards.

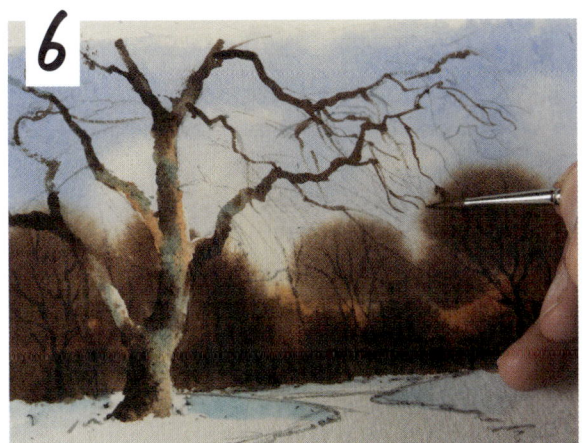

6

▶ Once they are in place, begin to add the finer branches, which do droop downwards, using the same mix and the tip of the size 2 brush.

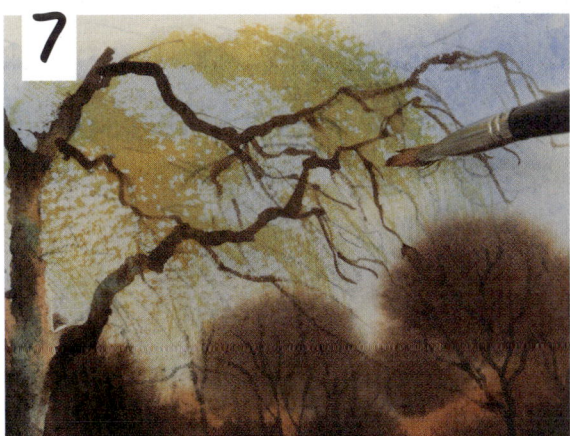

7

▶ Prepare a mix of cadmium yellow and light red. Pick the colour up on the 6mm (¼in) flat and use sweeping, downward curving strokes to establish the fine twigs and leaves stemming from the fine branches.

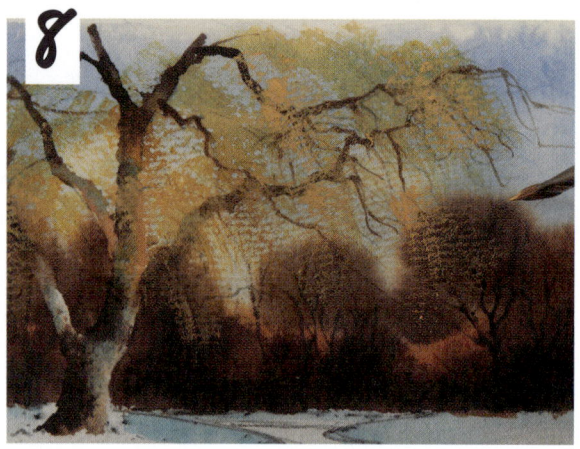

▶ Still using the 6mm (¼in) flat, build the effect by applying pure Naples yellow with the same sweeping, downard curving strokes. This technique will gradually obscure the underlying branches.

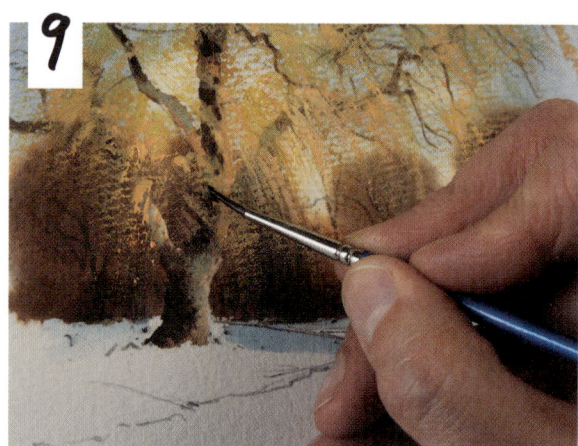

▶ Using the dark mix (French ultramarine and burnt sienna), re-establish a few areas where the trunk and branches show through, using the size 2 round. This helps prevent the tree looking flat.

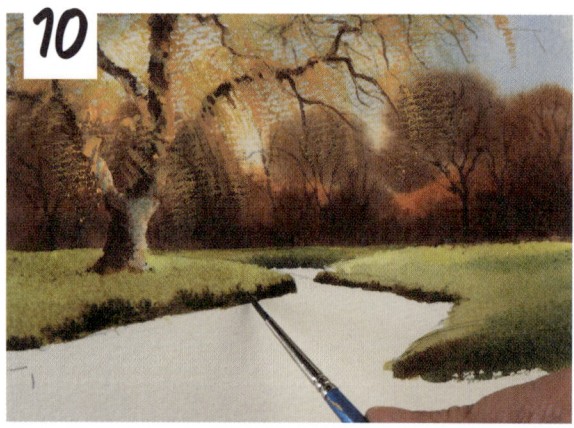

▶ Once the tree is completed, you can remove the remaining masking fluid from the riverbanks and paint them using an olive green mix of cadmium yellow and cobalt blue; and a dark green mix of viridian, French ultramarine and burnt sienna.

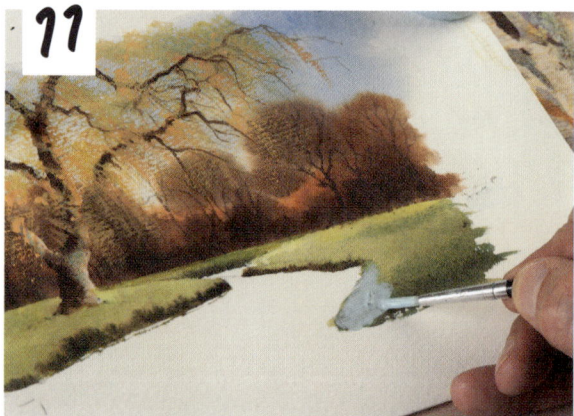

▶ Once completely dry, add another layer of masking to the riverbank where it curves back in on itself.

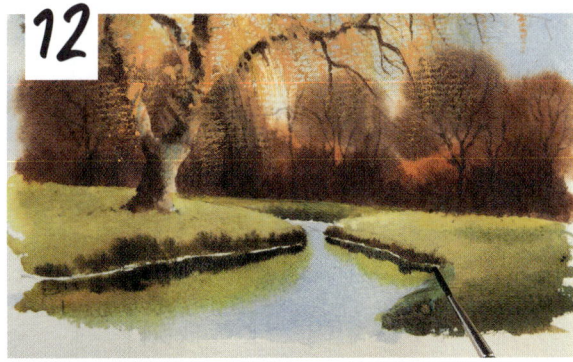

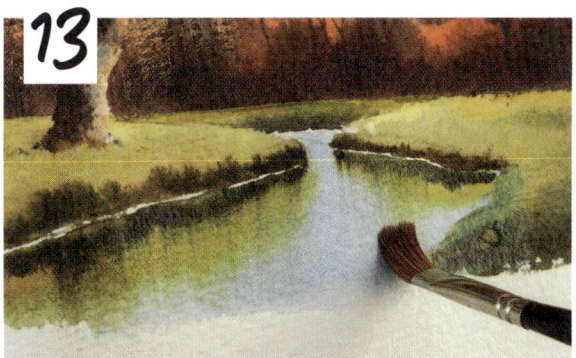

▶ Once the masking is set, wet the river area with clean water and paint in the river water using the sky mix (cobalt blue and French ultramarine) and the size 4 round brush. Drop in bands of olive green (cadmium yellow and cobalt blue) and dark green (viridian, French ultramarine and burnt sienna) wet-in-wet.

▶ Make sure your 6mm (¼in) flat brush is clean and dry and use it to lightly stroke the paint downwards to suggest the reflections. From here, finishing the painting is as simple as removing the masking fluid once the paint has dried.

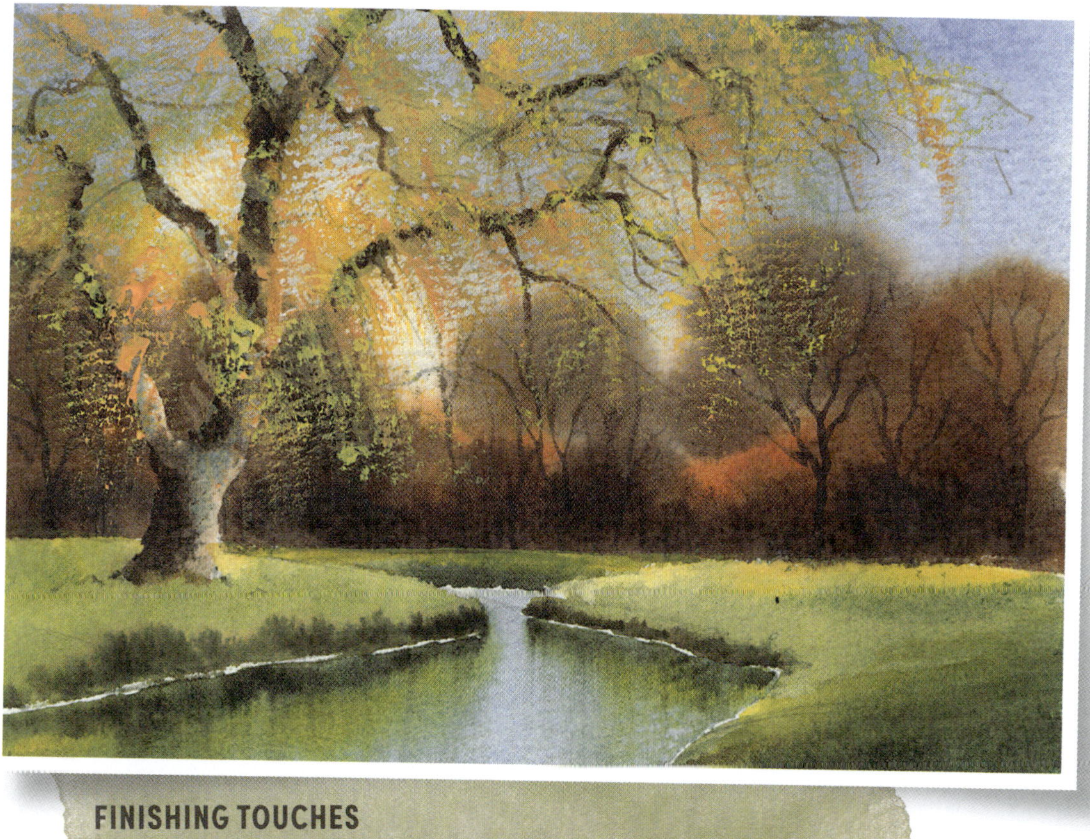

FINISHING TOUCHES

If the masking takes a little of the paint with it, you can reapply the paint – this is much easier than not masking and having to clean up any vertical streaks from the flat brush.

Parkland in Autumn

Shadows are important to create the impression of form. As well as shadows that appear on the trees themselves, remember that the trees will cast shadows on the areas around them. This project will let you practise suggesting the lay of the land.

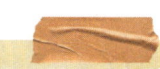

YOU WILL NEED

Paint colours: quinacridone gold, aureolin, cobalt blue, viridian, French ultramarine, burnt sienna, lemon yellow, rose madder, Naples yellow

Brushes: masking fluid brush, size 16 round, size 6 round, size 4 round, size 2 round, size 10 round

Other: masking fluid, bar of soap, outline drawing on page 90 (bottom)

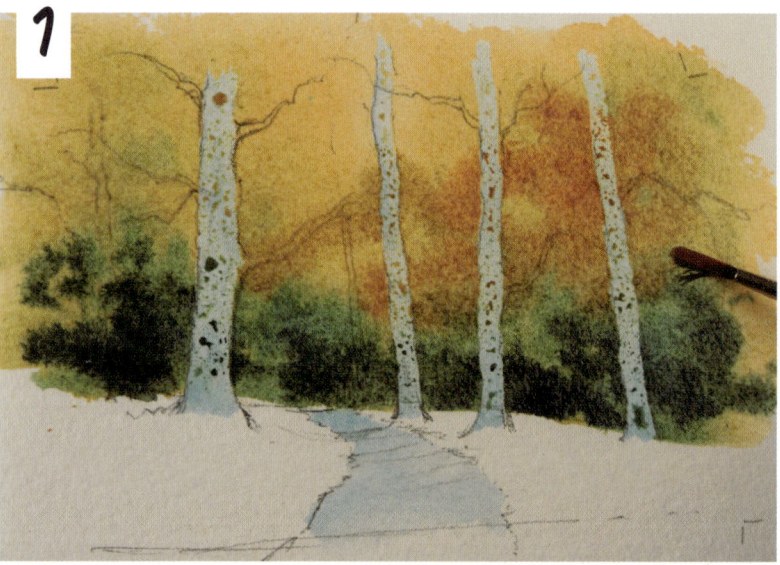

▶ Mask out the path and the trees as shown. Once dry, paint the background with a variegated wash: start with quinacridone gold, then, working wet-in-wet, add a bright green mix of aureolin and cobalt blue, and a blue-green made from cobalt blue and viridian. Keep these additions nearer to the middle and bottom of the area. Drop in a dark green mix of viridian, French ultramarine and burnt sienna using a size 4, adding these touches right at the bottom. Warm the quinacridone gold by adding burnt sienna and drop in some touches across the middle and top of the wet background area, then allow it to dry.

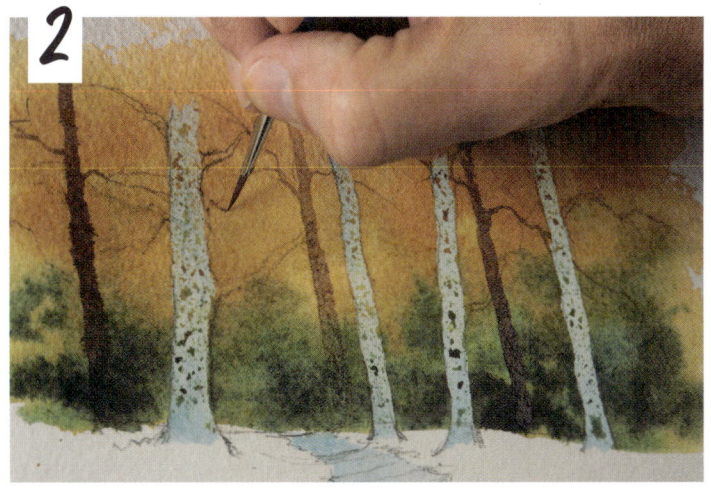

▶ Add the distant trees using the size 2 round and a grey mix of cobalt blue, rose madder and burnt sienna. Vary the consistency to create a sense of recession. Use the tip of the brush to add fine branches to the background trees with similar consistencies to their trunks. You can create particularly distant trees by using a very dilute version of the mix and applying the paint with the side of the brush. This will create faint, broken lines.

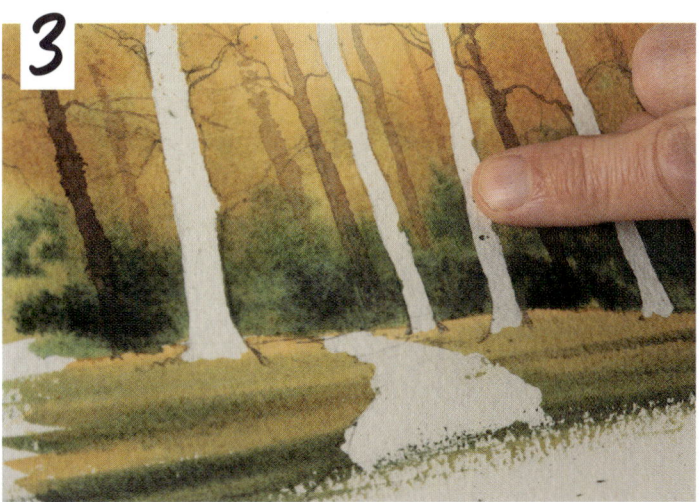

▶ Paint the grass using a size 10 round and the orange mix of quinacridone gold and burnt sienna to add horizontal strokes. Introduce the bright green (aureolin and cobalt blue) below that wet-in-wet, then more of the orange mix at the bottom. Add some dark areas with the dark green mix (viridian, French ultramarine and burnt sienna). Once dry, remove all of the masking fluid with a clean finger.

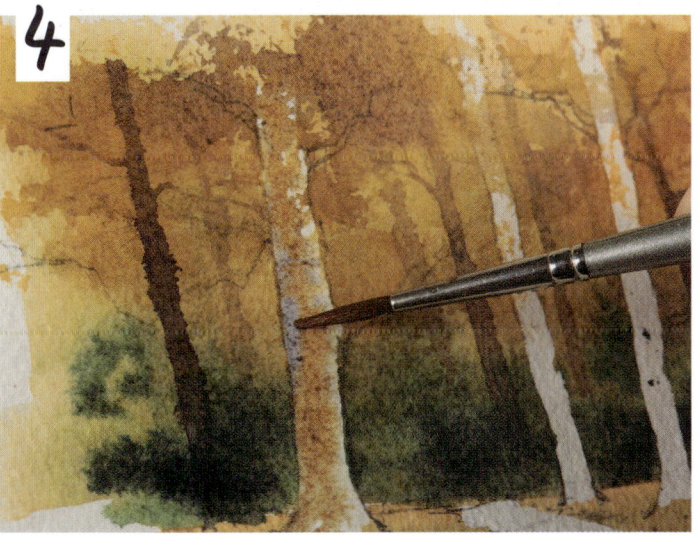

▶ Begin painting the foliage using the dry brush technique and the size 6 round to apply a purple mix of rose madder and cobalt blue around the top of the painting. Repeat the process with the orange mix, then a mix of lemon yellow and quinacridone gold.

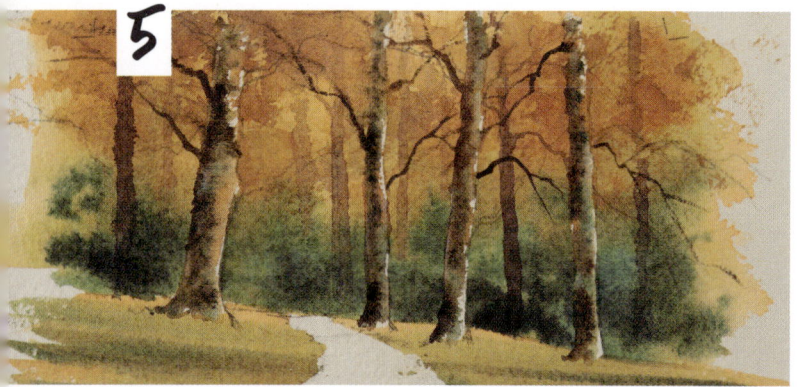

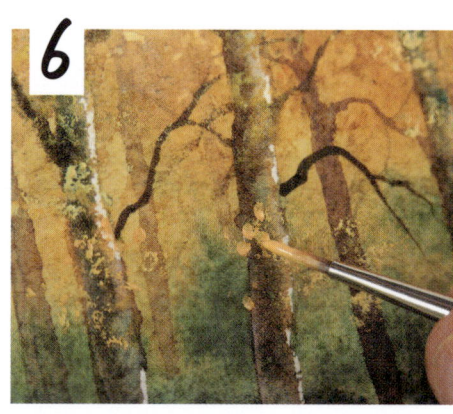

▶ While the foliage is wet, add the shadow mix with a size 4 round to the trunks of the trees; then add the orange mix wet-in-wet. Add more burnt sienna to the dark green mix to make it strong and dark and use this wet-in-wet to shade the trunks further. Leave white on the right-hand sides for highlights, and break up the strokes near the tops to fit in around the foliage. Use the tip of the size 2 round to add fine branches with the dark mix as you work. Some of these should cross the distant trees in order to help the viewer place the larger trees in front.

▶ Allow to dry, then add autumnal leaves in front of the trees using a mix of Naples yellow and quinacridone gold, applying the paint with the size 6 brush and the dry brush technique. Pick out some larger highlights of the same mix with the tip of the size 2 brush.

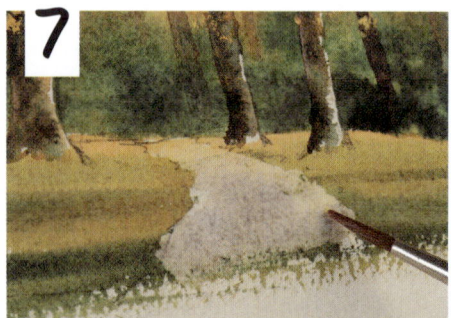

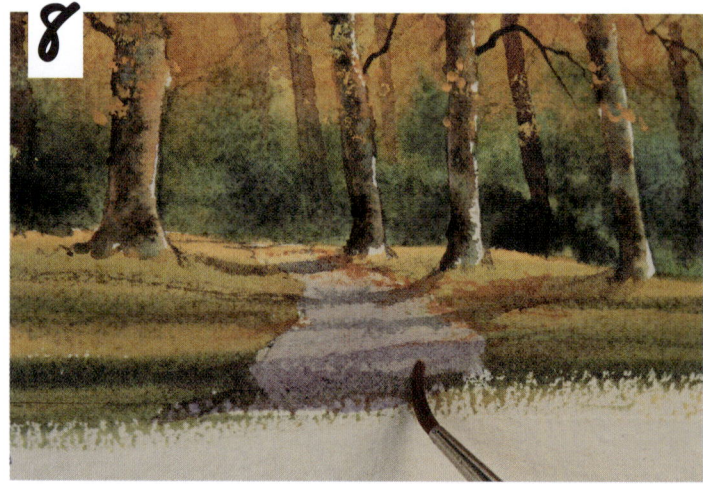

▶ Add the path with a dilute mix of quinacridone gold, with a mix of cobalt blue and rose madder added wet-in-wet.

▶ Once dry, add the suggestion of scattered leaves on the edges of the path using the tip of the size 2 brush and a mix of burnt sienna and quinacridone gold; and then some stronger purple shadows across the grass and the path using the size 4 round.

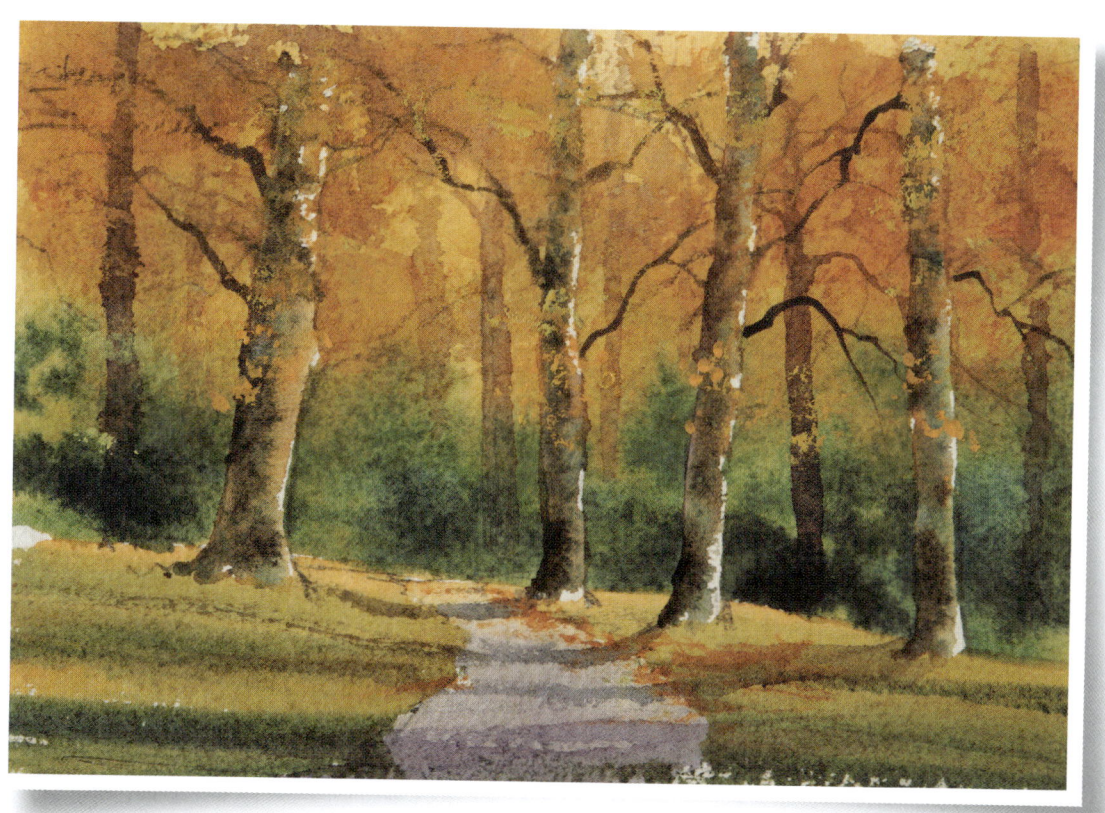

The finished postcard

Cherry Blossom

In this scene, you are not aiming to paint individual flower heads, but instead to create the impression of a mass of blossom. Swift but controlled wet-in-wet work is the key to success here. Preparing the paints in advance is a good idea, so read all the way through the instructions and make your mixes before starting the project.

YOU WILL NEED

Paint colours: cerulean blue, cobalt blue, aureolin, opera rose, cobalt violet, white gouache, burnt sienna, French ultramarine, rose madder, lemon yellow

Brushes: size 16 round, size 10 round, size 6 round, size 4 round, size 8 round, size 2 round

Other: outline drawing on page 91

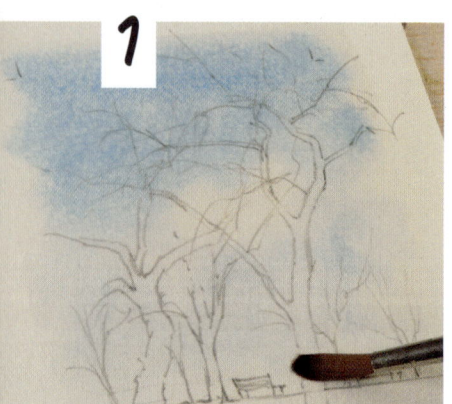

▶ Start by wetting the top two thirds of the painting with clean water, using the size 16 round brush. Drop in a sky wash of cerulean blue mixed with a little cobalt blue using the size 10, working down from the top. Weaken the colour with more water towards the bottom of the wet area.

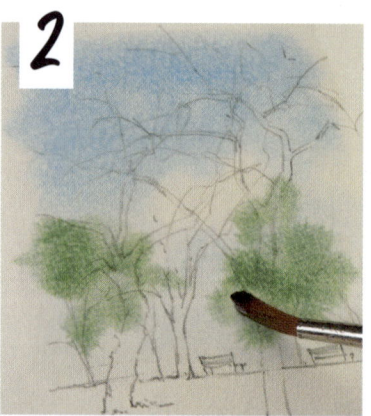

▶ Make a green mix of aureolin and cobalt blue – this is slightly thicker and has relatively more blue than the other green mixes in the book – and drop it in wet-in-wet.

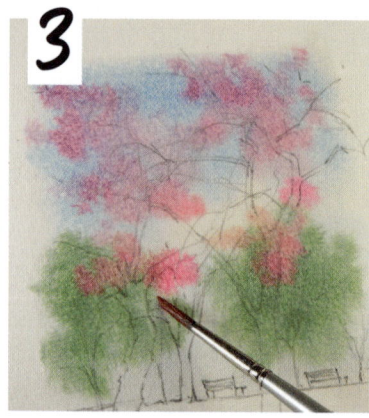

▶ Change to a size 6 round. Working down from the top of the tree, start dropping small touches of opera rose into the wet paint.

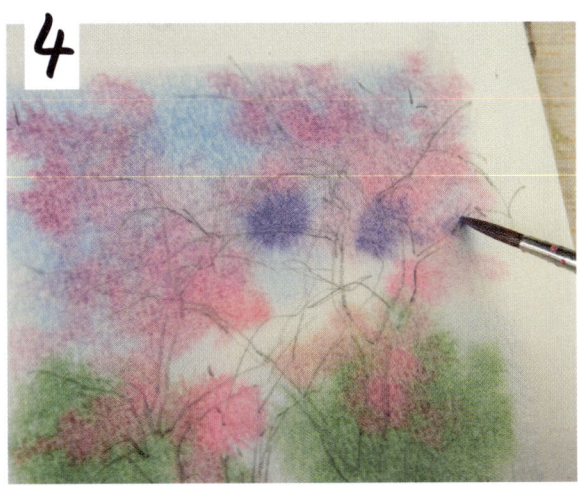

4

▶ Continue adding more opera rose as you work down the tree, including into the green areas. Drop in touches of a purple mix of cobalt violet with cobalt blue wet-in-wet, to create variety and interest.

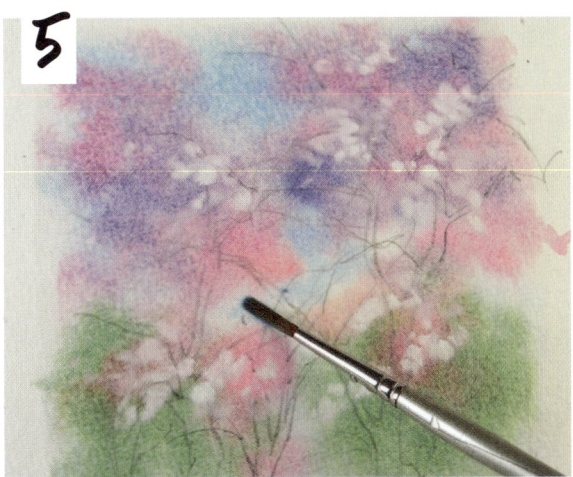

5

▶ Working rapidly, change to a size 4 round and pick up some pure white gouache. Use the tip of the brush to add tiny touches in and among the pink and purple.

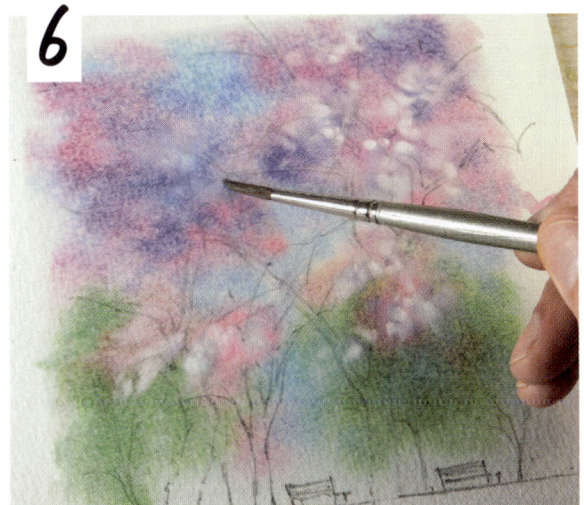

6

▶ If any of the opera rose area needs muting, to calm the effect a little, add a hint of the sky mix wet in wet. Soften any overly white areas with more of the purple mix. Allow to dry.

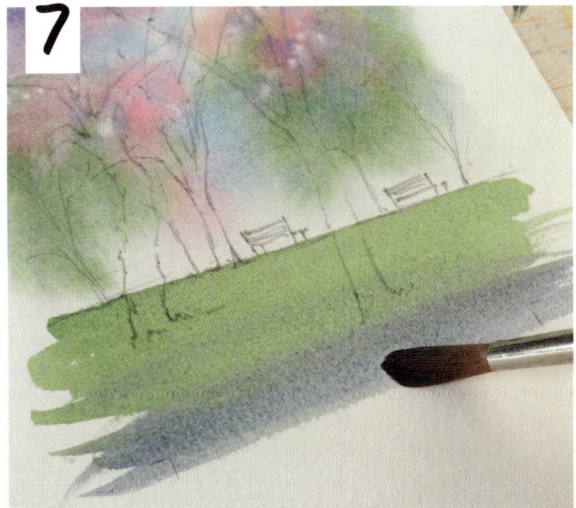

7

▶ Using a size 10 round brush, bring the green mix across the middle distance. Work right over the trees, and introduce some of the purple mix right at the bottom of the picture.

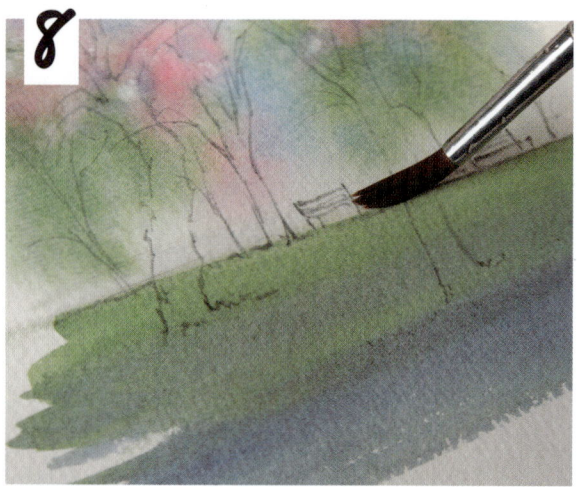

▶ Once dry, run a damp size 8 back and forth along the horizon to soften the edge. Be sure to retain a little of the bright area between the ground and the blossom.

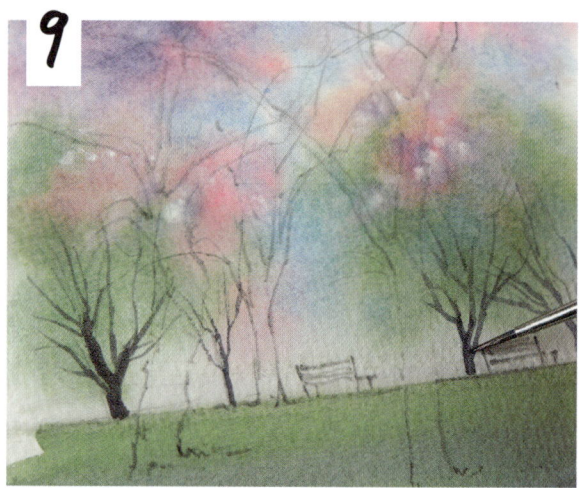

▶ Change to the size 2 round brush and use a grey mix of cobalt blue, cobalt violet and burnt sienna to paint the background trees. You can experiment with different tones for the trees; just remember that more distant trees will be paler in tone and appear smaller than those in the middle distance.

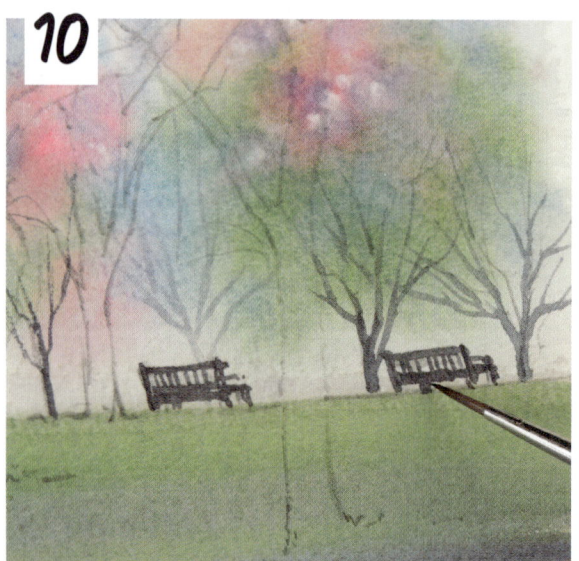

▶ Paint the park benches with the same mix and brush.

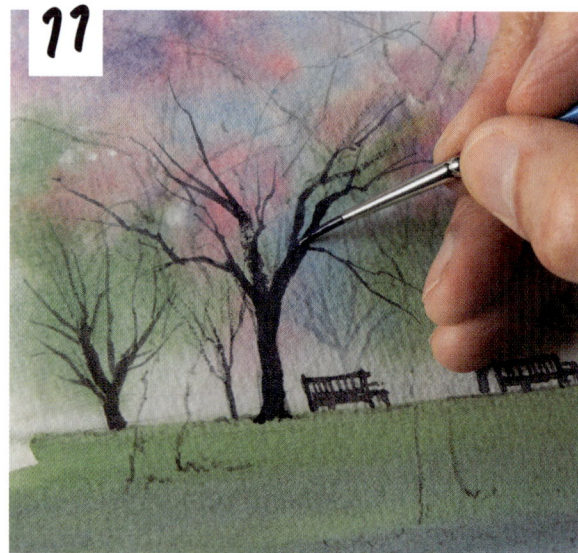

▶ Still using the size 2 round brush, strengthen the grey mix (cobalt blue, cobalt violet and burnt sienna) by adding more of each colour to the well, then begin to paint the foreground cherry trees, using this stronger tone. Start with the most distant and work forwards.

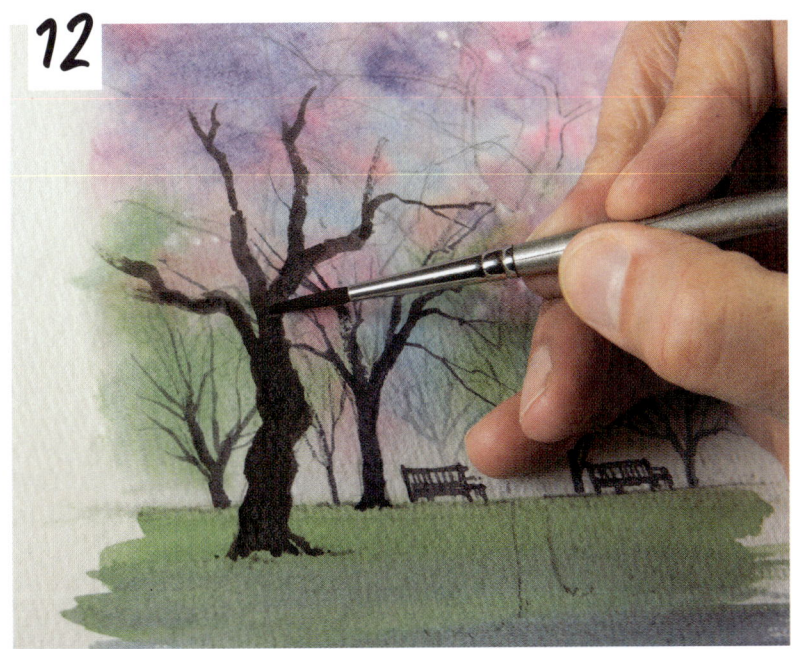

12

▶ For the foreground cherry trees, change to a mix of burnt sienna and French ultramarine with a touch of rose madder. Using the size 4 round brush, pay more attention to the gnarled shapes of the trunk and the angles of the main branches. Swap back to the size 2 brush to add finer branches which taper away to nothing in the mass of blossom.

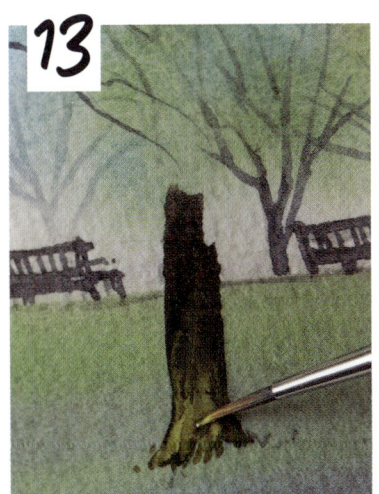

13

▶ Build up the foremost tree in the same way, adding a little neat lemon yellow wet-in-wet at the base of the trunk.

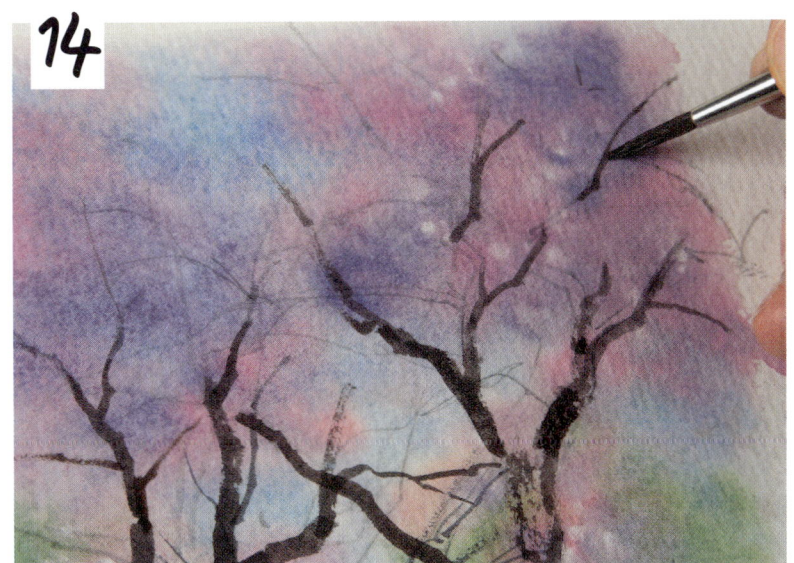

14

▶ Work upwards from the trunk. Use a slightly drier brush and leave gaps when painting the lines for the main branches, so they break up and appear partly obscured by the blossom.

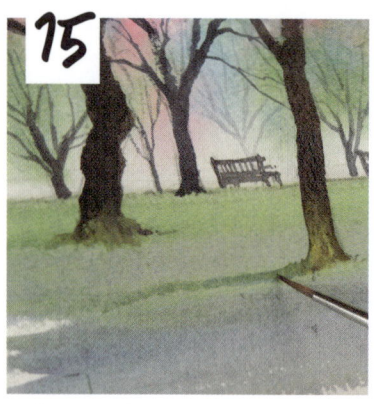

▶ Change to the size 2 round brush to soften the bases of the trees, and add some subtle cast shadows using the sky mix.

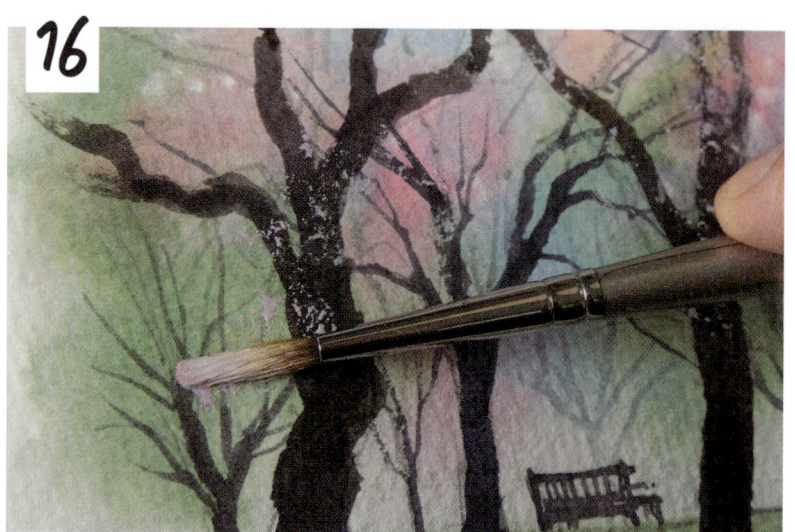

▶ Change to the size 4 round and add a tiny amount of cobalt violet to opaque white. Use the dry brush technique to apply it to the foreground tree. Add opera rose to the mix for variety.

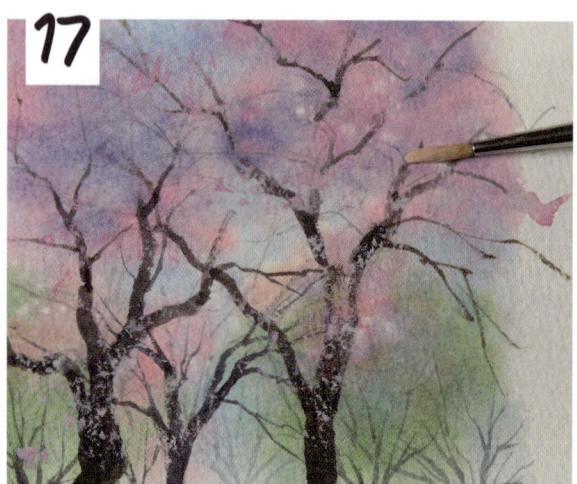

▶ Continue building up the blossom using the opaque mixes, then add some of the purple mix (cobalt violet and cobalt blue) in the same way, to create a shaded area.

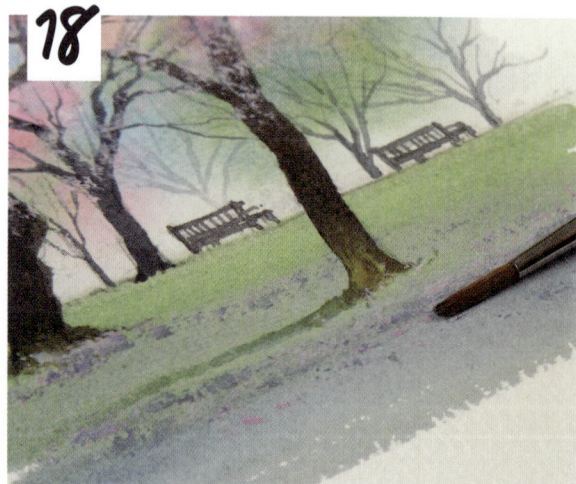

▶ Finally, add some marks sparingly across the foreground grass. Step away for a few minutes before returning to the painting with fresh eyes. You may feel that you want to add some additional blossom on the tree or on the grass beneath it.

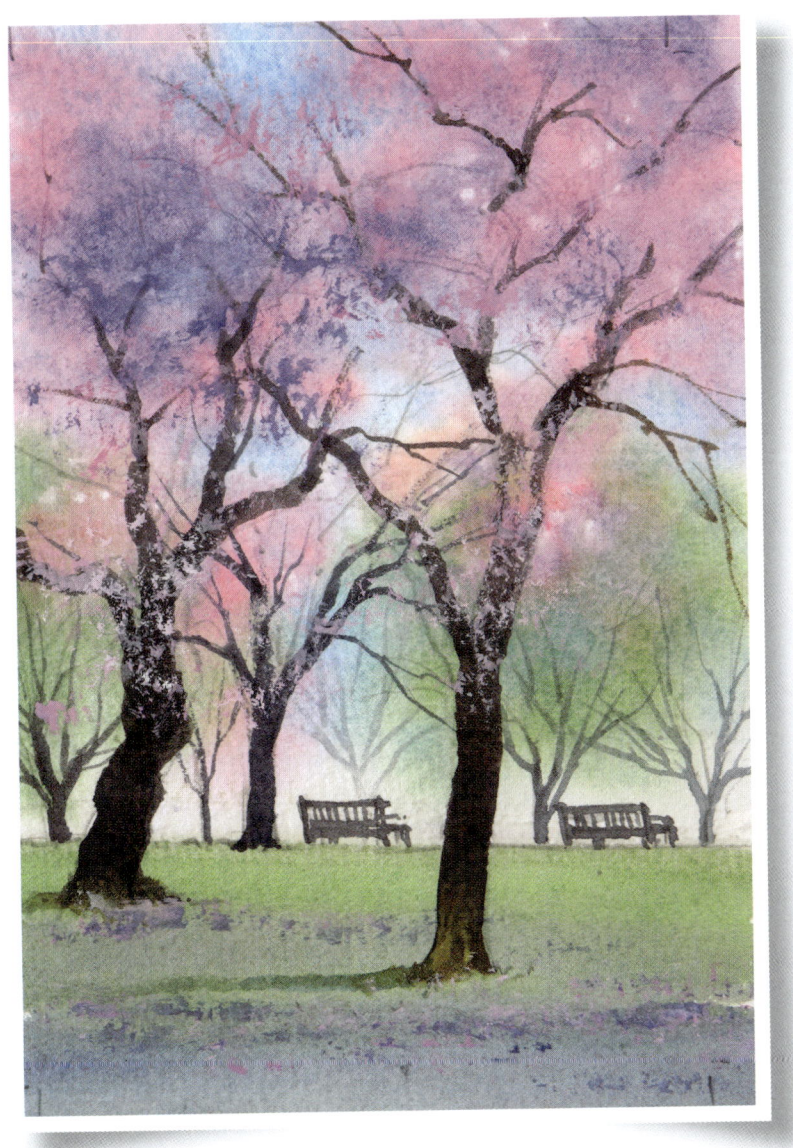

The finished postcard

Dappled Sunlight

The purple and orange colours used in this painting are complementary. When they are combined they turn an attractive grey; however, when placed next to each other unmixed, they set each other off, causing both to appear more vibrant. As you paint the foliage, look for areas where you can place these two colours close together without them mixing. This will increase the vibrancy of your picture.

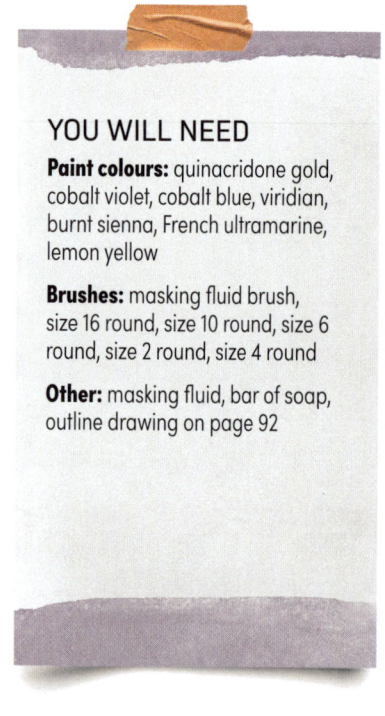

YOU WILL NEED

Paint colours: quinacridone gold, cobalt violet, cobalt blue, viridian, burnt sienna, French ultramarine, lemon yellow

Brushes: masking fluid brush, size 16 round, size 10 round, size 6 round, size 2 round, size 4 round

Other: masking fluid, bar of soap, outline drawing on page 92

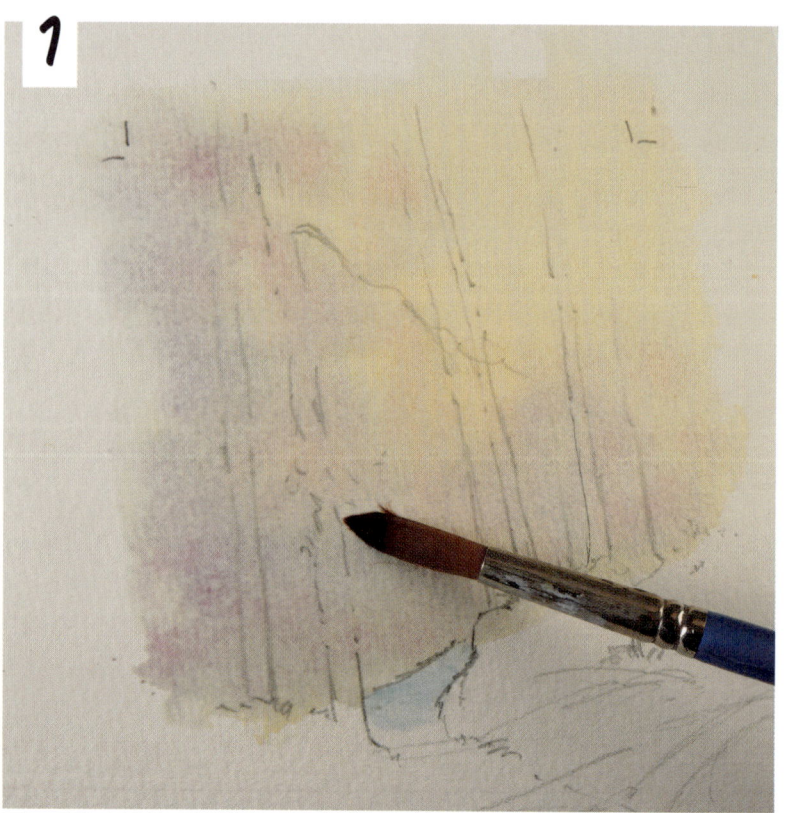

▶ Mask the path, wet the whole top two-thirds of the painting with the size 16 round brush, then switch to the size 10 round. Use this to paint the area with a thin wash of quinacridone gold, then add a purple mix of cobalt violet with a little cobalt blue wet-in-wet, concentrating it behind the trees and on the lower left, leaving the top right area with a warm glow.

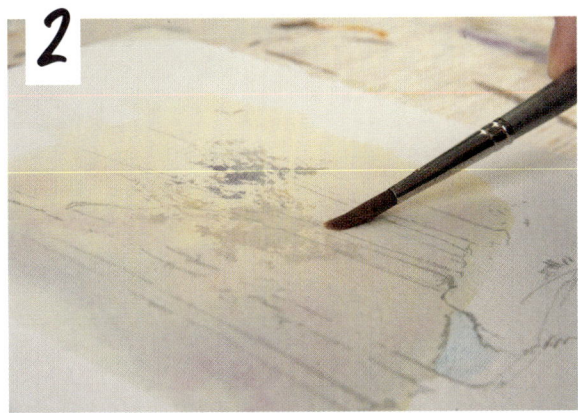

▶ Allow to dry. Mix viridian with cobalt blue to make a blue-green mix; and quinacridone gold with burnt sienna for an autumnal copper-red mix. Indicate broken foliage using the size 6 round, the dry brush technique and the cobalt violet and cobalt blue mix.

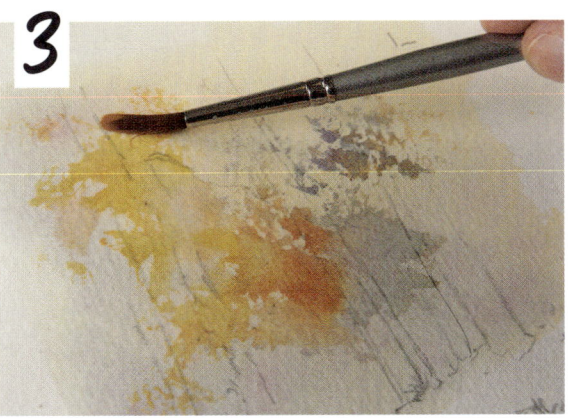

▶ Add the copper red mix and dilute lemon yellow towards the centre, then gradually introduce the blue-green mix. Where the paper is dry, you will get harder dry brush marks, but where parts remain slightly damp, you will get a softer wet-in-wet appearance.

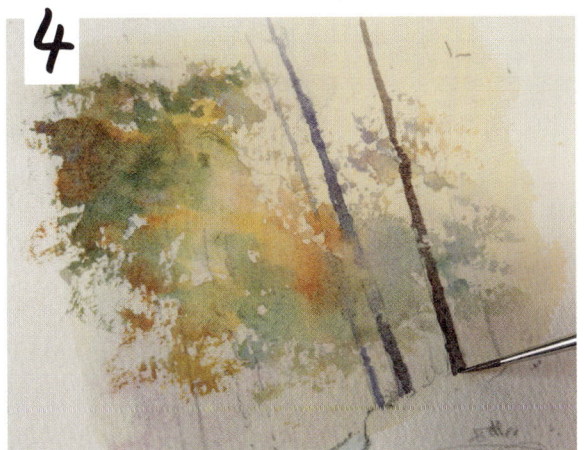

▶ Continue building up the foliage, concentrating cooler, lighter tones on the right-hand side, and stronger, warmer tones towards the left. Without waiting for the paint to dry, pick up the cobalt violet and cobalt blue mix on a size 2 round brush and begin to add the trunks of the trees. Dilute the paint for more distant trees, and break the lines a little to suggest intervening foliage.

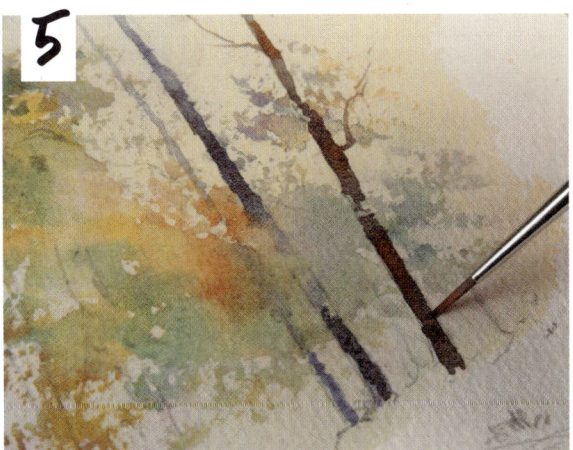

▶ Add burnt sienna to the mix for closer trees, with quinacridone gold wet-in-wet for warmth. You can add touches of this on the still-wet midground trunks to help 'bridge the gap' between the foreground and background trees.

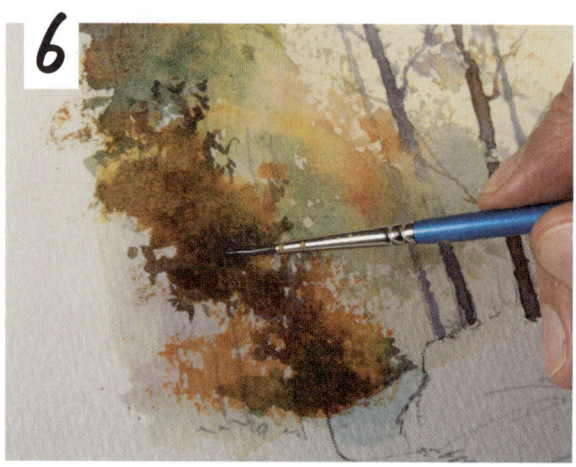

▶ Continue building up the trees, adding fine branches with tapering strokes of the size 2 round. Use the dry brush technique to apply the copper-red mix with the size 4 round to the area above the masked-out path. Touch in the cobalt violet and cobalt blue mix, and an orange mix of quinacridone gold and burnt sienna with a size 2 round while the colour remains wet.

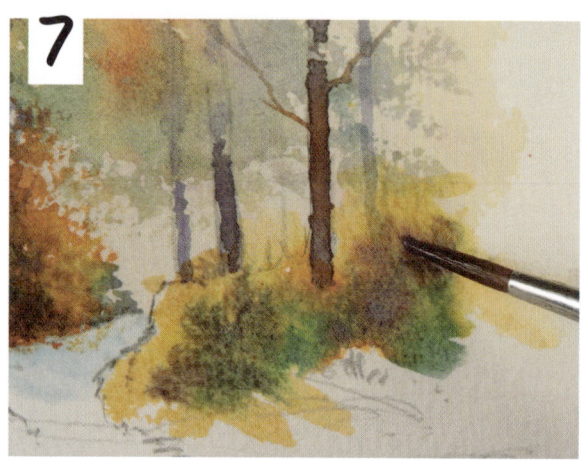

▶ Use the size 4 round to apply the orange mix and build up the bank on the right-hand side of the painting down to the path, dropping in the purples and greens on your palette, and adding hints of yellow wet-in-wet.

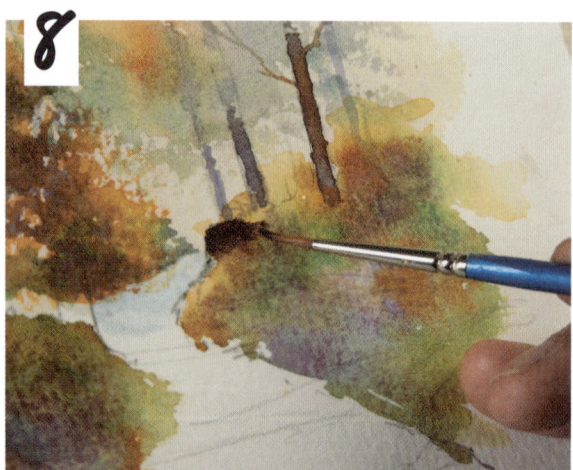

▶ Paint the left-hand bank in the same way using the mixes on your palette. Allow the painting to dry, then mix burnt sienna and cobalt blue. Use a size 2 round brush to paint the large rock on the right-hand bank. The top edge should be sharp, but soften the bottom into the bank with a clean damp brush.

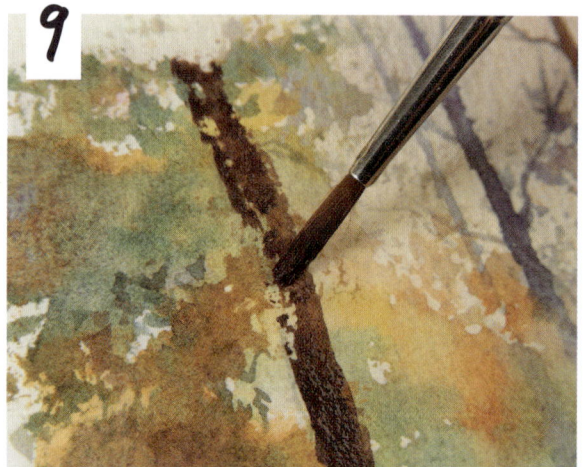

▶ Mix burnt sienna with French ultramarine and cobalt violet for a warm dark. Paint in the largest tree trunk with a size 4 round brush. Dash it in fairly quickly, allowing the colour to break up towards the top of the stroke. Rinse the brush and soften the roots into the bank with the damp bristles.

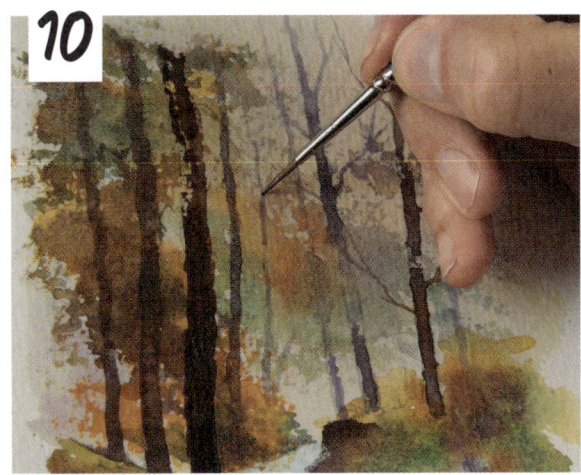

10

▶ Dilute the mix and repeat the process for the foreground trees to the left of the main tree, then add some faint background trees with a diluted cobalt blue and cobalt violet mix.

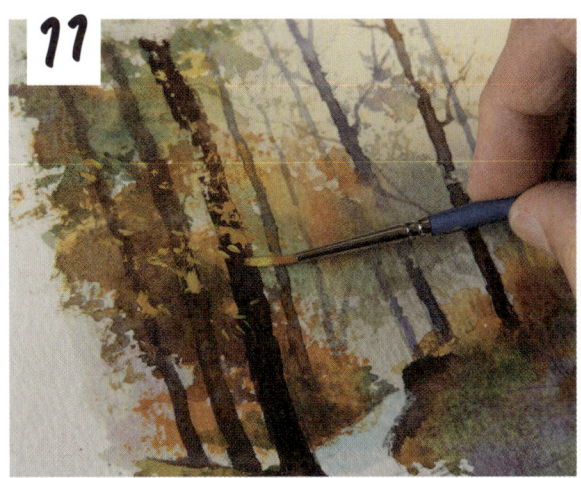

11

▶ Mix lemon yellow with quinacridone gold to make a warm opaque yellow-orange. Use this to hint at leaves on the left-hand side with the tip of the brush and also with some dry brush work.

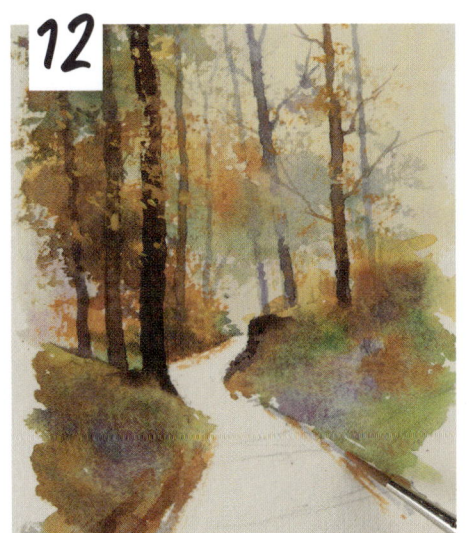

12

▶ Continue this over the right-hand side, using just dry brush work – these trees are too distant for the individual leaves to 'read'. Remove the masking fluid, then break up the edges of the path with the same warm yellow-orange mix, to prevent it looking too clean and sharp. Allow the painting to dry before going any further.

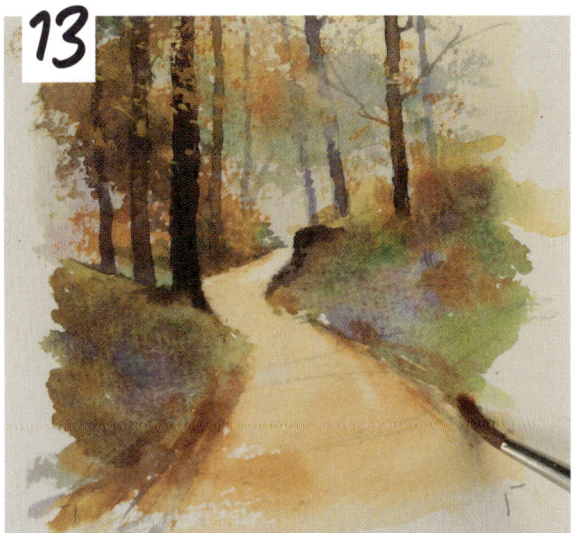

13

▶ Switch to a size 4 round and wet the area where the masking was. Change to a size 6 and wet the remainder of the path, working over the broken edges you have just established. Add a dilute mix of quinacridone gold and burnt sienna, concentrating the subtle colour towards the bottom of the painting and leaving the distant path light. Allow to dry.

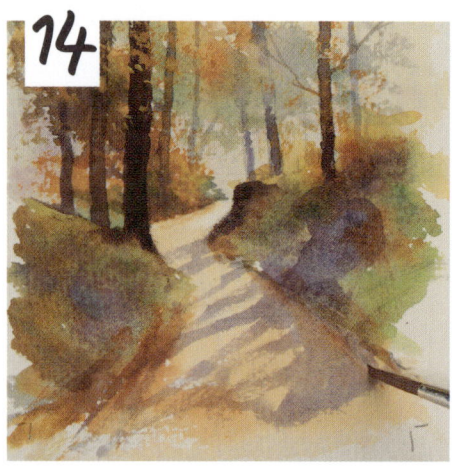

▶ Use the cobalt blue and cobalt violet mix to paint in shadows that work down the bank and across the path, creating a dappled mass of shadow with the size 6 round.

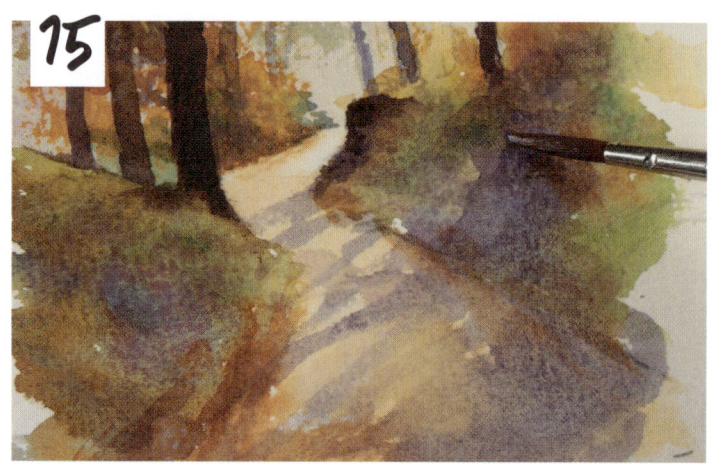

▶ Rinse the brush and soften the colour a little with the damp bristles, then introduce a little burnt sienna wet-in-wet at the bottom right of the painting.

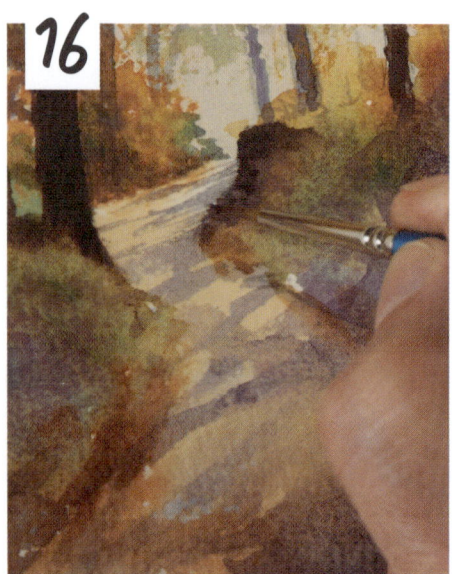

▶ Use the size 2 round to add some fine shadows on the distant path.

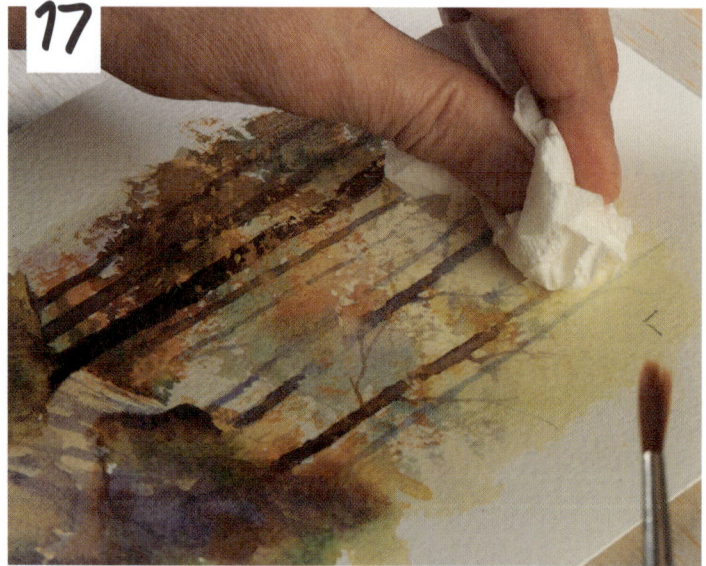

▶ Use a wet size 6 round to dampen the top left of the painting and use a piece of kitchen paper to lift out some of the colour.

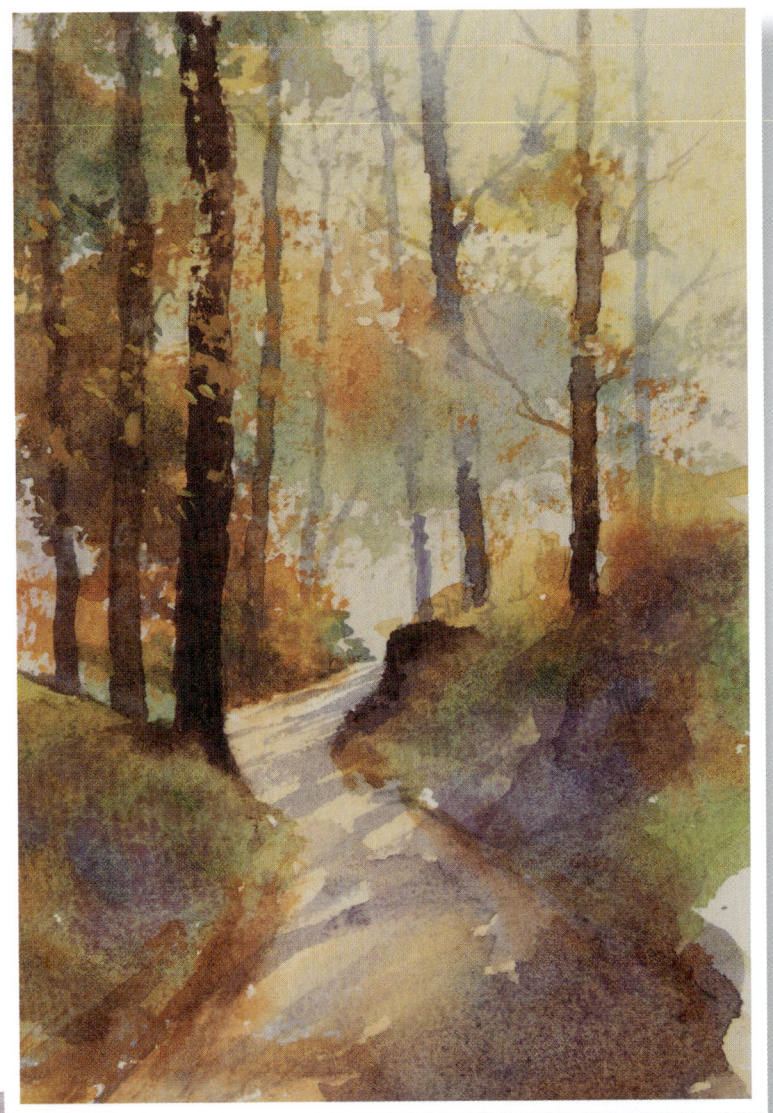

FINISHING TOUCHES

Make any tweaks and refinements you like to finish your postcard,
but be careful not to overwork it – the bright atmosphere relies on a
light touch.

Looking into the Light

This project gives you practice in using shadows to describe the contours of the landscape, and can also be useful for emphasizing perspective. Notice how the converging lines of the shadows lead the viewer's eye past the foreground trees and into the woods. You should always guard against making shadows too strong, as it should appear as though you can see the land beneath them, through the transparent colour.

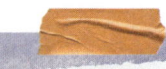

YOU WILL NEED

Paint colours: Naples yellow, light red, cobalt blue, rose madder, burnt sienna, raw sienna

Brushes: masking fluid brush, size 16 round, size 10 round, size 2 round, size 6 round, size 4 round

Other: masking fluid, bar of soap, craft knife, white gouache, outline drawing on page 93

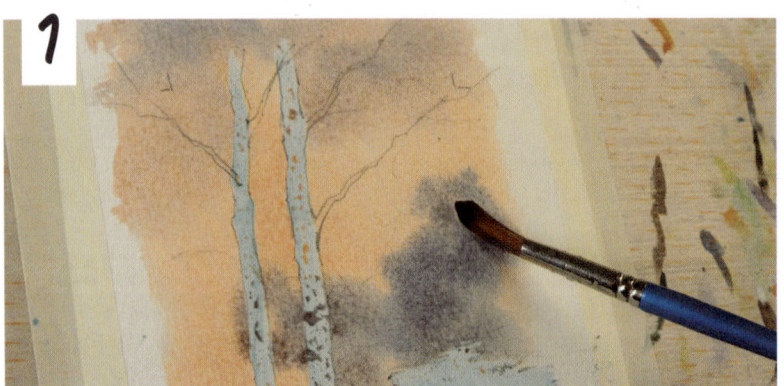

▶ Mask out the main trees and the sloped area where the land meets the woods. Wet the background from the top down to the masked-out bank using the size 16 round brush. Use the size 10 round to drop in a wash of an orange mix made from Naples yellow and light red over the whole background. Working wet-in-wet, add a thin purple wash of cobalt blue and rose madder at the top, then drop in a grey mix of cobalt blue, rose madder and light red further down to represent background trees.

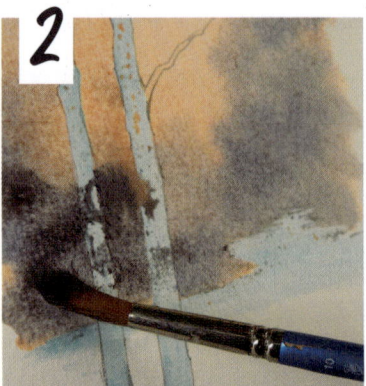

▶ Add a dark mix of cobalt blue, burnt sienna and rose madder wet-in-wet at the base of the trees using light, dabbing, textural touches with the size 10 brush.

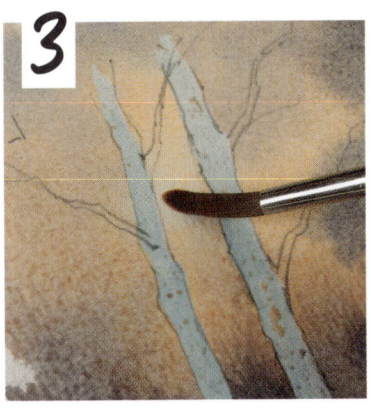

▶ Clean and dry the brush and lift out a little colour from the centre, behind one of the trees. This is the light source.

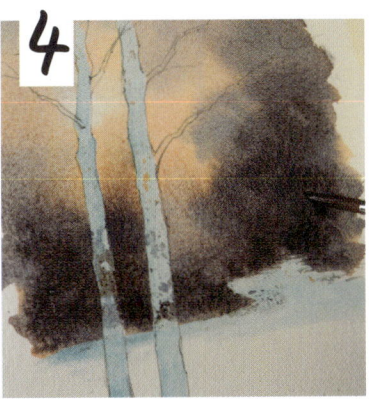

▶ Add a little more of the dark mix in wet-in-wet around the edge of the woodland, then allow the painting to dry.

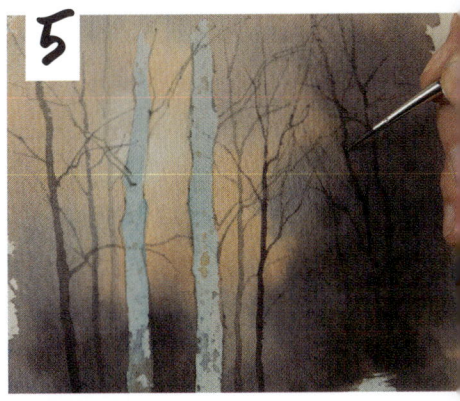

▶ Use the size 2 round brush to add some background trees using the grey and brown mixes. Vary the intensity of the tone by adding water (or more paint) in order to create variety among the trees and suggest that some are further away than others.

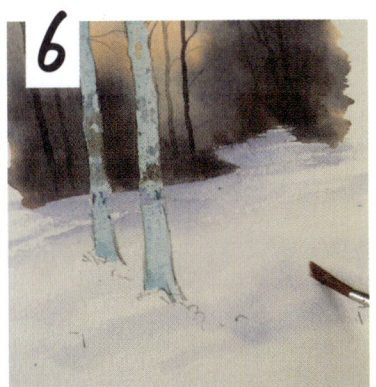

▶ Remove the masking fluid from the woodland, but leave it on the main trees. Use a dilute mix of cobalt blue and rose madder to add quick, light shadows over the revealed area with the size 6 round. Soften the brushstrokes in on the bank itself to create a smoother effect.

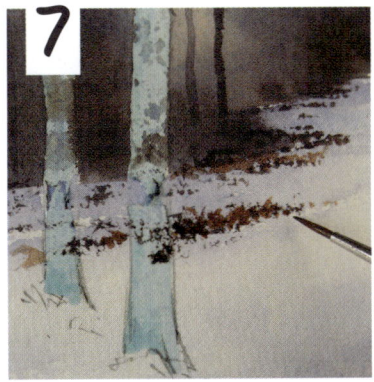

▶ Use the dark mix (cobalt blue, burnt sienna and rose madder) fairly strongly to suggest stones and weeds on the snow using the size 2 round brush and the dry brush technique. Keep these marks close to the wooded area (not across the whole foreground) and angle them so they follow the slope. Add raw sienna and burnt sienna to the mix to warm and vary it.

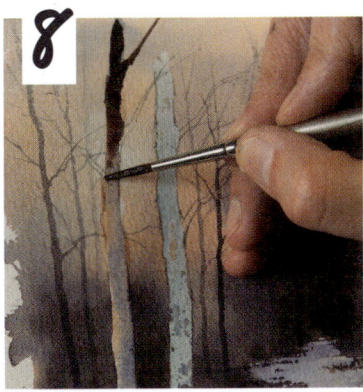

▶ Remove the masking fluid from the tree on the left and use the size 4 brush to paint it with the orange wash, before dropping in the grey mix (cobalt blue, rose madder and light red). While it is still wet, bring in some of the dark mix from the top, working down from the edge of the painting into the tree.

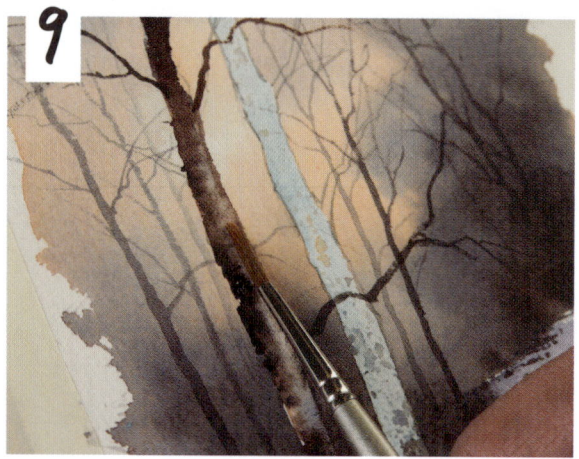

▶ Change to a size 2 round brush and add smaller details on the bark and a few fine branches with the same mix. Lift out a little of the wet paint on the front of the tree trunk using a clean, dry size 4 brush.

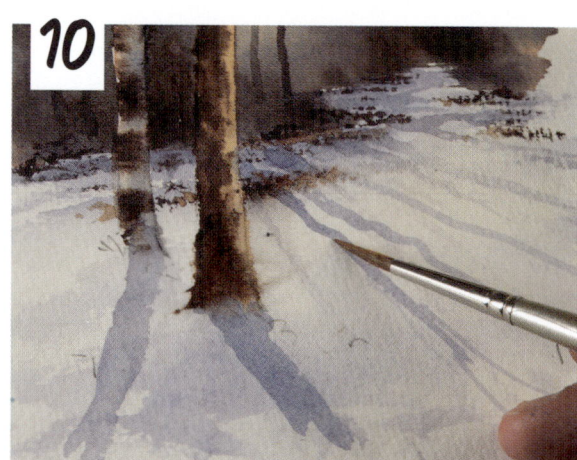

▶ Remove the masking fluid from the second tree and paint it in the same way. Once complete, use the purple wash (cobalt blue and rose madder) and the size 2 round brush to add some cast shadows to the foreground. These should extend from the bases of the trees, and point directly away from the light source (see step 3).

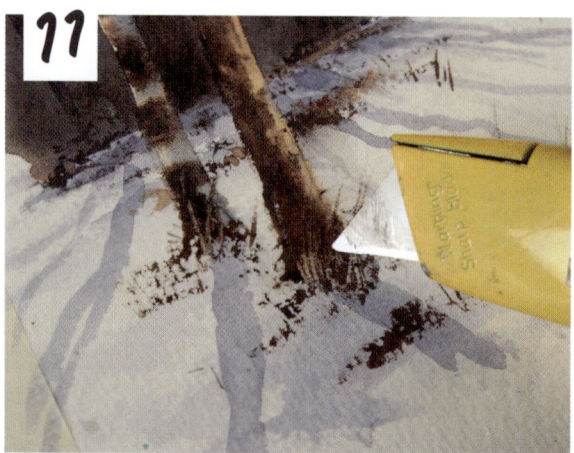

▶ Use the brown mix and the size 2 round brush with the dry brush technique to add some details around the base of the trees, then use the point of the brush to add a few flicking strokes to suggest grasses. While the paint remains wet around the base of the trees, use the blade of a craft knife to lightly flick the paint up and scratch out the colour.

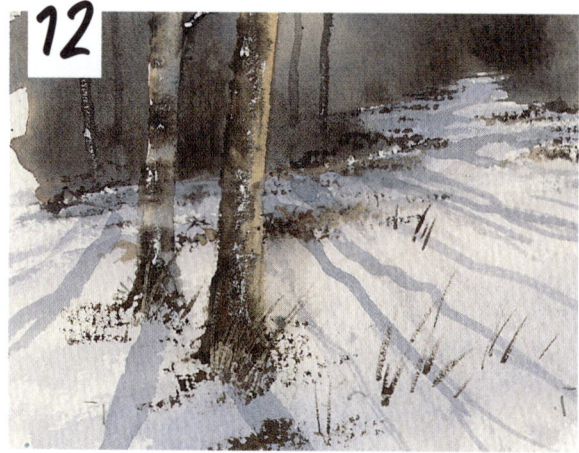

▶ To enhance the effect, wet a size 4 round brush and re-wet the light source, then lift out a little more paint with some clean kitchen paper. Once dry, restrengthen the silhouette of the right-hand tree with the point of the size 2 round and the dark brown mix. Finally, add a few touches of white gouache as eye-catching flecks of snow.

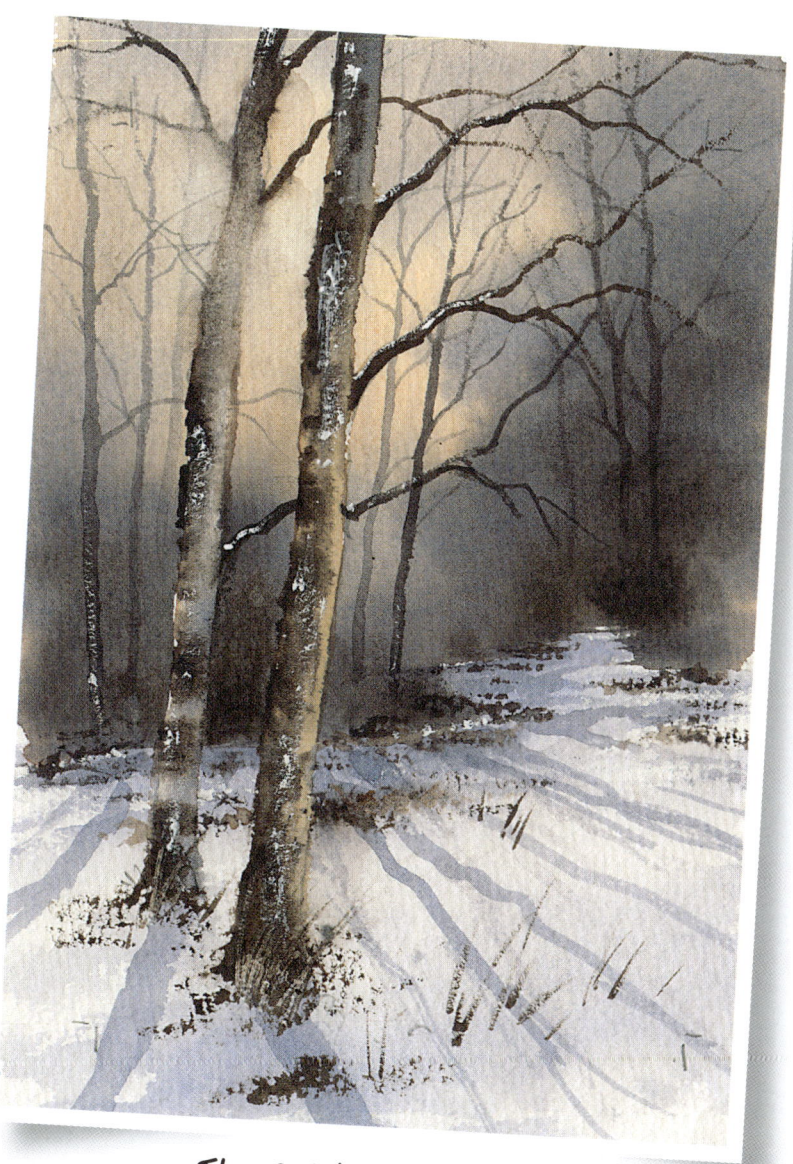

The finished postcard

Fir Trees

In addition to learning how to paint pine trees, this project will show you how to use trees to frame the scene and lead the viewer's eye into the painting. When painting firs, keep any yellow touches sparing; fir trees are mainly cooler blue-greens, and too much yellow can make them stand out as unusual.

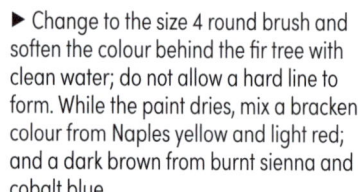

YOU WILL NEED

Paint colours: cobalt blue, light red, raw sienna, Naples yellow, burnt sienna, viridian, French ultramarine, lemon yellow

Brushes: masking fluid brush, size 10 round, size 4 round, size 2 round

Other: masking fluid, bar of soap, outline drawing on page 94 (top)

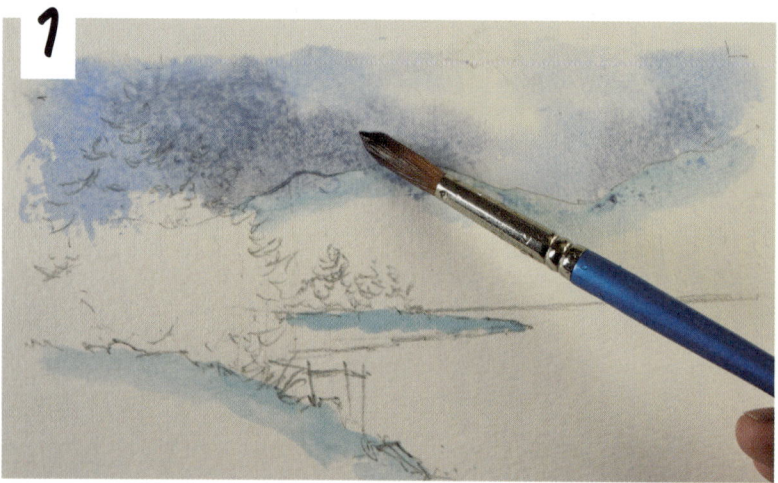

▶ Mask out the crest of distant hills and the peninsula on the lake, plus the area under the trees. Wet the sky down to the hills with the size 10, then drop in cobalt blue. Working wet-in-wet, drop in a grey mix of cobalt blue and light red, particularly near the mountains.

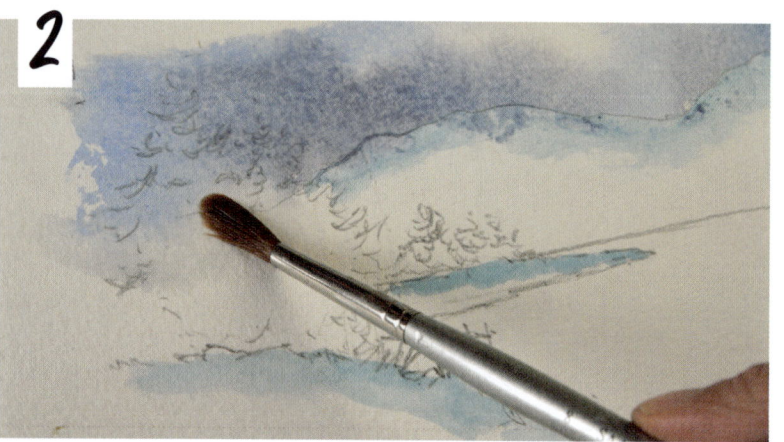

▶ Change to the size 4 round brush and soften the colour behind the fir tree with clean water; do not allow a hard line to form. While the paint dries, mix a bracken colour from Naples yellow and light red; and a dark brown from burnt sienna and cobalt blue.

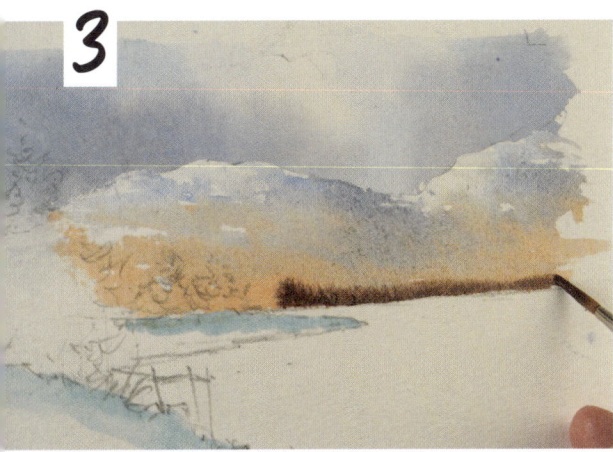

▶ Once dry, remove the masking fluid from the hills with a clean finger. Using the dilute cobalt blue and the grey mix you used in the sky, add shadows to the hillsides, applying the paint and then drawing it out with a damp size 4 brush. Leave a few white patches for the snow, and keep the darker areas on the right-hand sides of the hills. As you work down, introduce the bracken colour, and then the dark brown towards the water's edge.

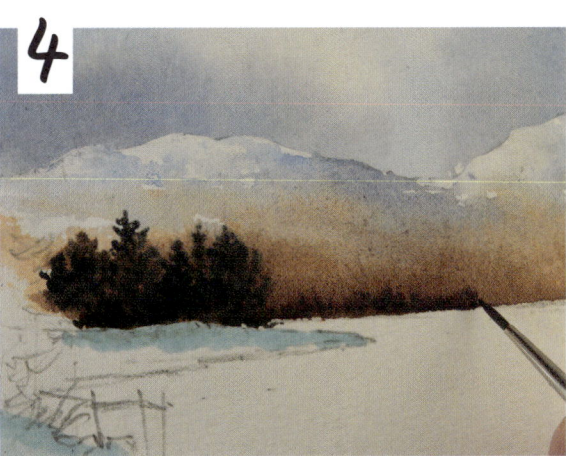

▶ Working wet-in-wet with the brown mix, use tiny flicks of the size 2 round brush to introduce a mass of distant firs on the far side of the lake. Use a dark green mix of viridian, French ultramarine and burnt sienna to paint the firs, working each one down from their tips. Vary the size of the firs. Add more cobalt blue to the grey mix and touch this in on the water's edge to create a strong line.

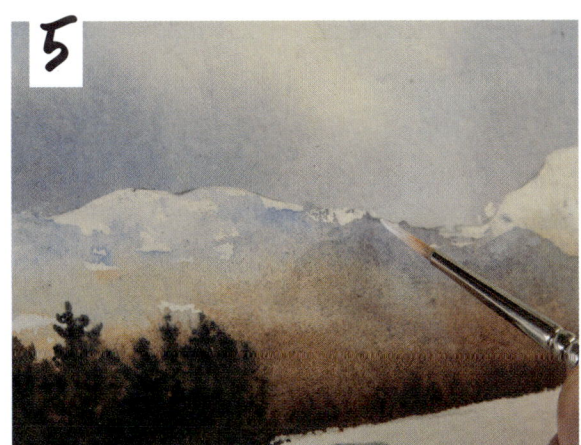

▶ Once dry, use the original grey mix (cobalt blue and light red) to give more definition to one of the hills. This has the effect of knocking one back into the distance, and bringing the other in front. If required, use a size 2 round brush to add some white gouache to reinstate the snow on the ridge. Don't go overboard – a few touches are enough.

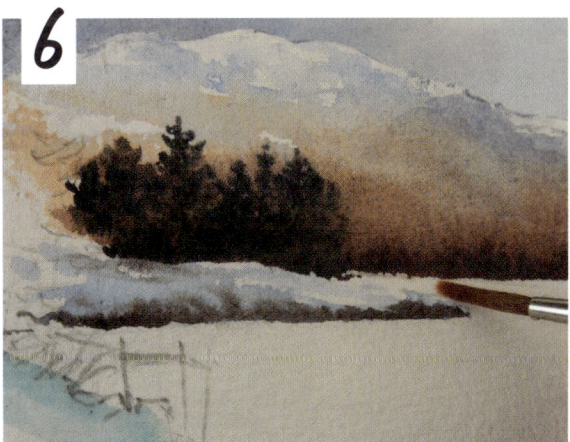

▶ Once dry, remove the masking fluid from the peninsula. Add some cobalt blue over the area, leaving a line of white below the fir trees. Touch in the grey mix near the water's edge, then draw a line of a second dark brown mix – burnt sienna and French ultramarine this time – across the edge while the grey remains wet.

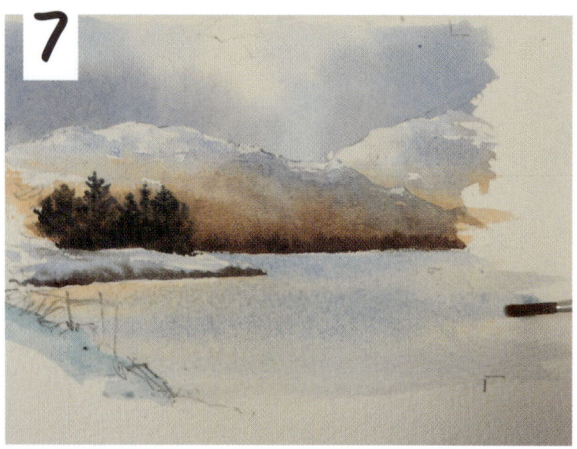

7

▶ Change to the size 4 brush. Taking care to keep clear of the peninsula, and leaving a fine line of clean dry paper by the banks, fill the lake with clear water, then add a few streaks of the peachy mix. Add dilute cobalt blue wet-in-wet, starting from the far edge and working downwards.

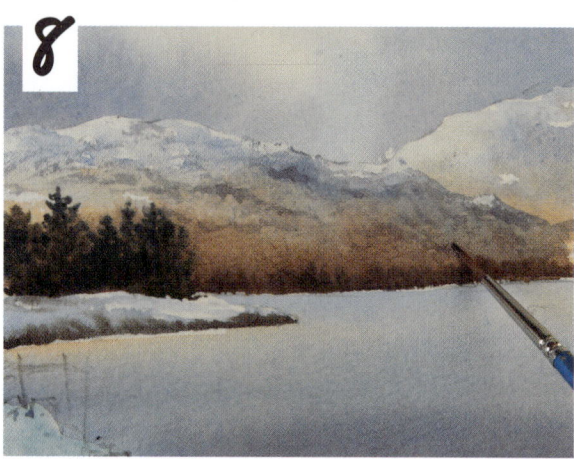

8

▶ Add some of the grey mix at the very bottom, again using horizontal strokes. Once dry, add some texture on the closer hillside using the tip of the size 2 brush and the grey mix (cobalt blue and light red).

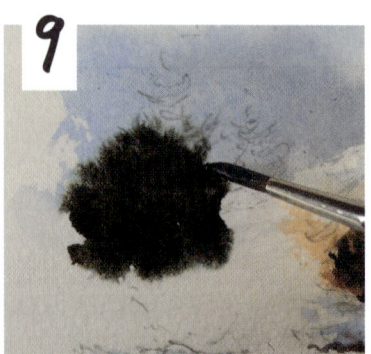

9

▶ Change to a size 10 round and re-wet the fir tree on the left, taking the clean water beyond the edges of the tree. Working upwards from the bottom, apply the dark green mix (viridian, French ultramarine and burnt sienna) with the size 6 round brush, working up and outwards from the lower centre. Use slight taps to apply the paint, to give a dappled texture to the result.

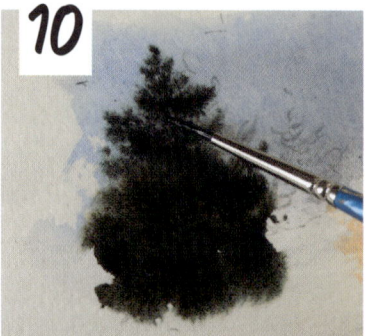

10

▶ Change to the size 2 and add the top part of the main fir in the same way, using similar strokes, but smaller and more controlled. These foreground firs frame the picture, providing the eye with an anchor to lead the viewer into the scene.

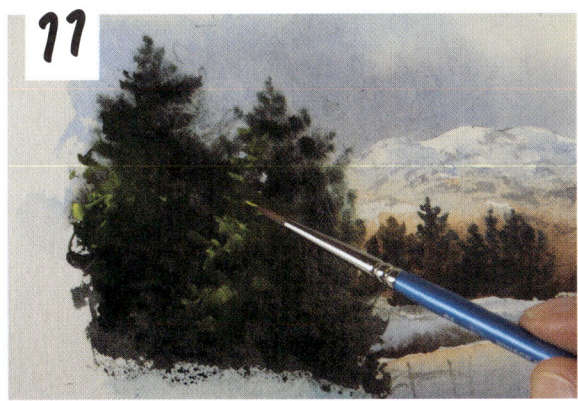

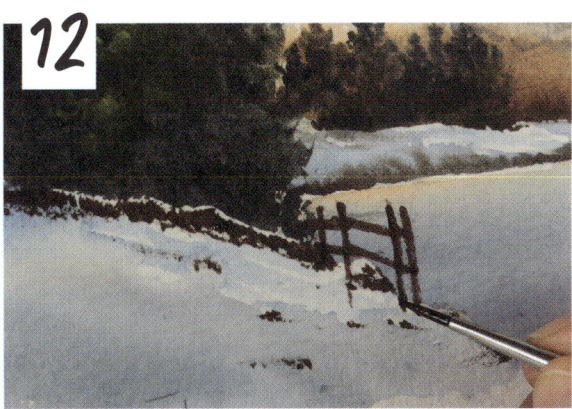

▶ Build up the smaller fir tree in the foreground in a similar way. The wetness of the area is important – if it bleeds so much that you are losing the shape of the branches, it is too wet; pause and wait for the paper to dry a little before continuing. To distinguish the trees, add a few small neat lemon yellow touches with the tip of the size 2 brush to the left-hand sides as shown.

▶ Once dry, remove the remaining masking fluid and paint the revealed corner with a cobalt blue and grey mix using the size 6 round. Details like the small wall in front of the foreground fir trees, scattered stones and fencing to the right of the trees can be added with the dark brown mix (burnt sienna and French ultramarine) and a dry size 2 round. Leave thin white lines to suggest snow on top of these details, and remember the shadows cast by the fencing.

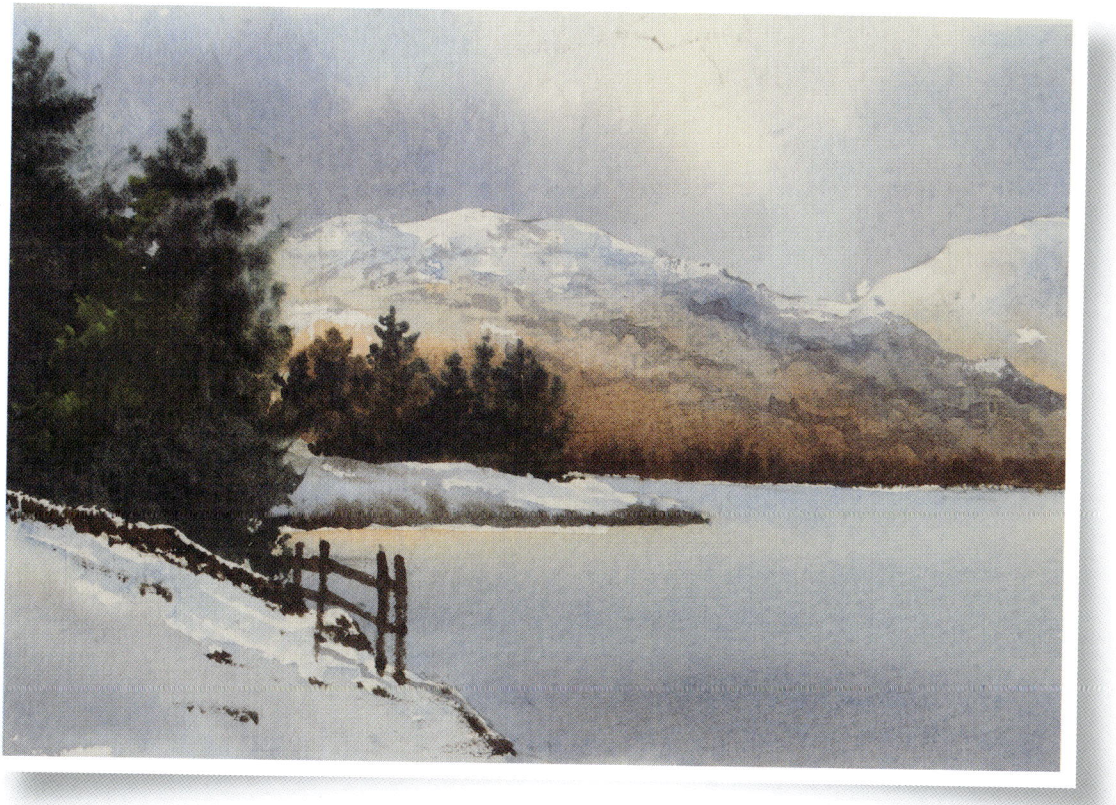

The finished postcard

Winter Lane

This project looks at recession along with the creative use of opaque white gouache. It is also a good example of the importance of making trees look individual. When adding the branches, try to avoid adding them directly opposite a branch coming from the trees on the opposite side. Even if one is there in real life, in a painting it can look contrived.

Opaque body colour (gouache) is usually applied to the dry surface to reinstate or create highlights, but here it works beautifully to create the softness of snow in the middle distance when applied wet-in-wet.

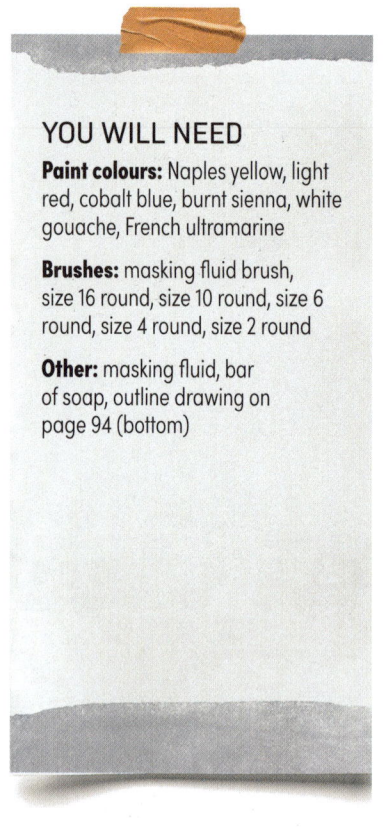

YOU WILL NEED

Paint colours: Naples yellow, light red, cobalt blue, burnt sienna, white gouache, French ultramarine

Brushes: masking fluid brush, size 16 round, size 10 round, size 6 round, size 4 round, size 2 round

Other: masking fluid, bar of soap, outline drawing on page 94 (bottom)

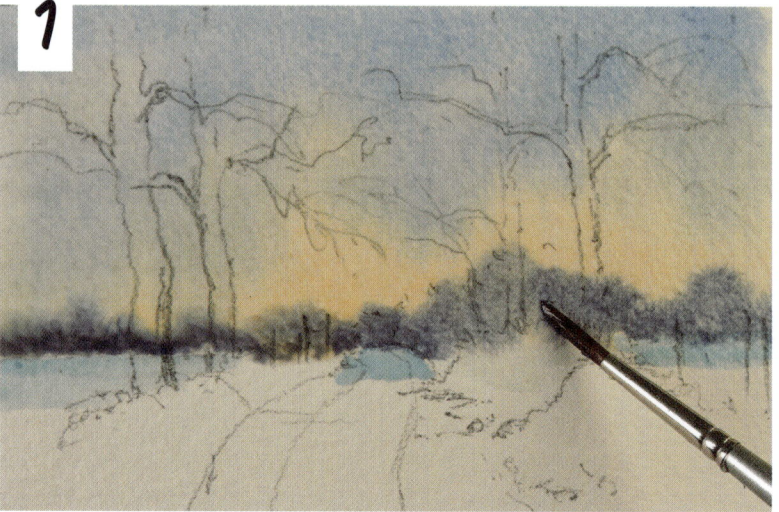

▶ Mask fine lines along the far left and far right of the horizon, and on the distant path. Wet the background down to the horizon line with the size 16 round, then drop in a very thin wash of a Naples yellow and light red mix above the horizon. Add thin cobalt blue wet-in-wet at the top. Allow the paint to dry a little, then drop in touches of a neutral grey mix made from cobalt blue and light red along the horizon with the point of the size 6 brush.

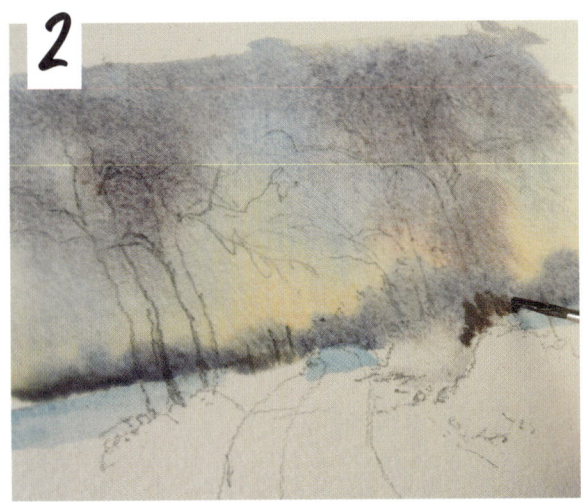

▶ Add some more red to the neutral grey mix to warm it, and drop it in around the tops of the trees. Switch to the size 4 brush and make a strong grey from cobalt blue and burnt sienna. Strengthen the colours around the base of the trees on the right-hand side.

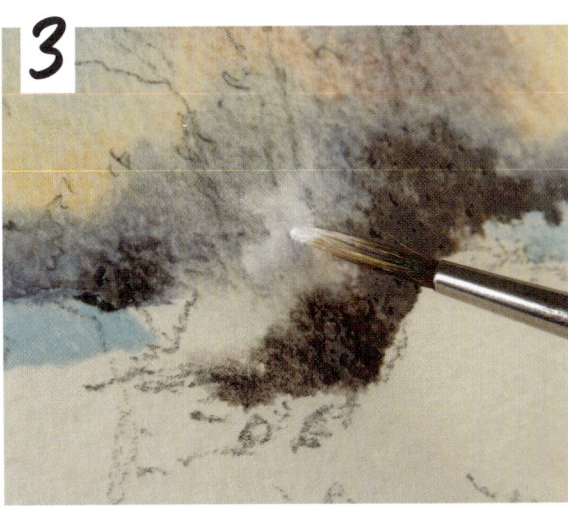

▶ Still using the size 4 round brush, add some touches of white gouache wet-in-wet over the lower part of the right-hand trees.

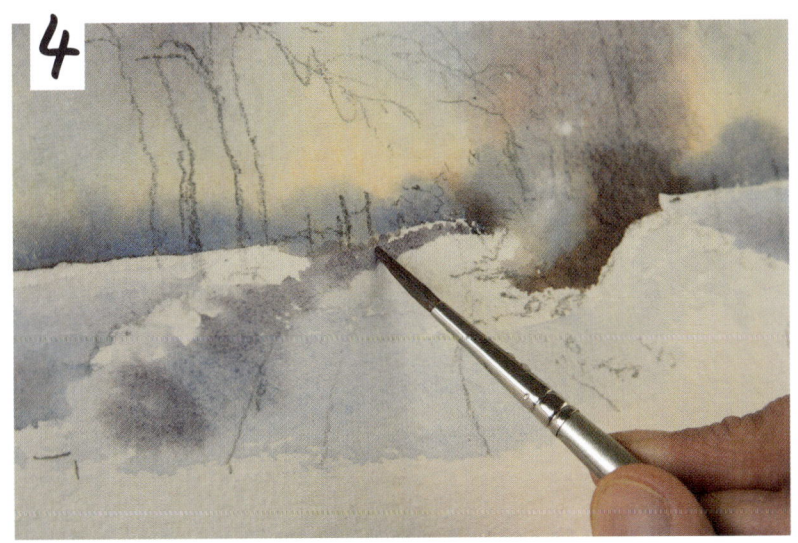

▶ Once dry, remove the masking fluid. Add snow shadows across the foreground fields on both sides using the thin cobalt blue wash and a size 6 round brush. As the area approaches the hedges, bring in the stronger neutral grey wet-in-wet. Add more tone to the lower part of the sky by wetting it with clean water and the size 6 round. Drop in neutral grey. Use the same brush to add dilute cobalt blue across the road, softening it in with clean water. Switch to the strong neutral grey to add some stronger tone and colour on the banks on either side of the road. Be careful to leave a thin sliver of clean white paper at the top – this is important to show the clean white snow on the top.

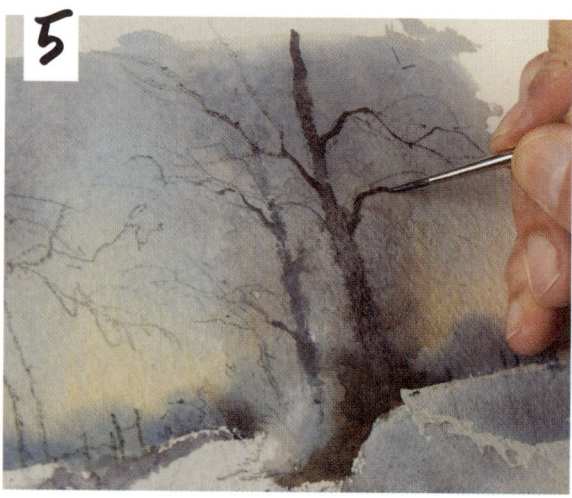

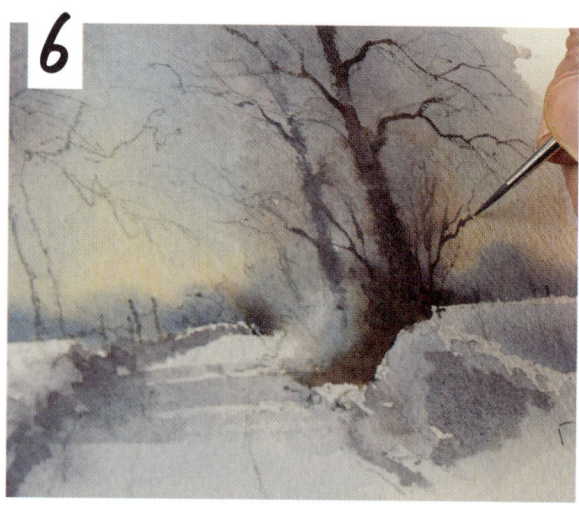

▶ With a strong mix of the neutral grey (add more cobalt blue and light red paint), use the side of the size 2 round to add a broken line to represent a background tree. Develop a few branches with the same mix, then strengthen the mix still further and repeat the process with the size 4 round brush for the larger midground tree on the right-hand side. Switch to the size 2 round for the main branches.

▶ Use the same mix to develop the foreground area with additional shading and cast shadows across the road. Apply these last with horizontal strokes. Use the very tip of the size 2 round brush to add the fine branches of the small bush in front of the large tree with the same mix.

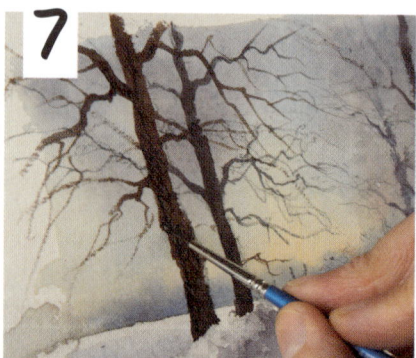

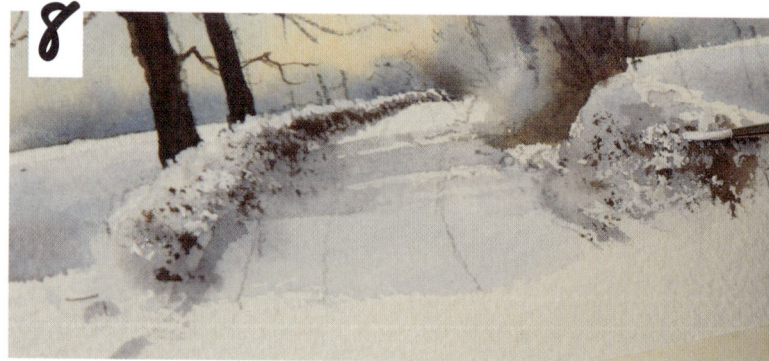

▶ Repeat the process with the tree on the left-hand side of the path, using a stronger grey mix made of burnt sienna and cobalt blue. For the leftmost tree, use a still stronger mix of burnt sienna and French ultramarine to make it appear a little nearer.

▶ Use a dry brush technique with the same mix for some foreground detailing around the hedgerow, using the size 2 brush on its side. Once dry, use the tip and side of the size 2 round brush to add touches of white gouache to refine the existing highlights in the foreground.

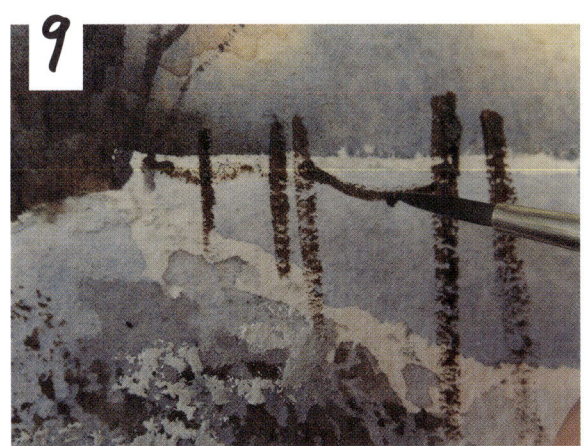

9

▶ Add subtle touches of snow to the main trees with white gouache, and a few fence posts and wire in the foreground with using the dark grey mix. Use a nearly dry brush for the posts, as the drag this creates will suggest a little texture.

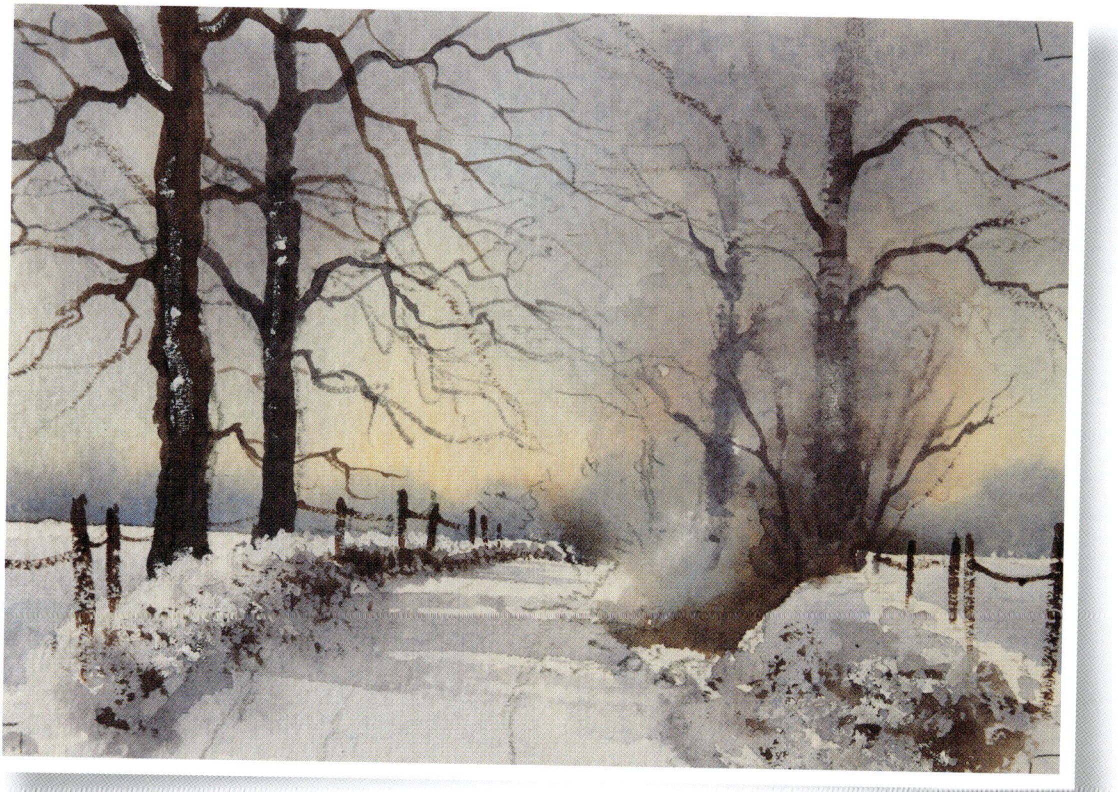

The finished postcard

Pond Reflections

The best way to create recession is to alter the tone – you can do this by adding more water to your mix for lighter, weaker tones and more paint for darker, stronger tones. This postcard painting also looks more closely at reflections.

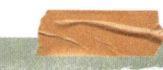

YOU WILL NEED

Paint colours: lemon yellow, aureolin, cobalt blue, viridian, cobalt violet, French ultramarine, burnt sienna

Brushes: masking fluid brush, size 16 round, size 10 round, size 6 round, size 2 round, size 4 round, 6mm (¼in) flat

Other: masking fluid, bar of soap, outline drawing on page 95

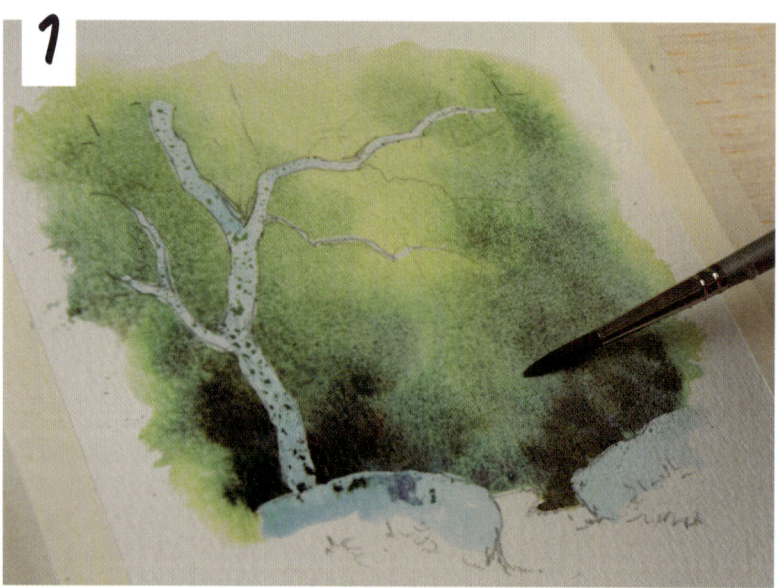

▶ Mask the main tree, large rocks and the water. Once dry, wet the background down to the masked-off rocks with the size 16 round brush. Use the size 6 brush to create a variegated wash of lemon yellow and a bright green mix of aureolin and cobalt blue. Add a green-grey mix of viridian and cobalt violet in around the lower half of the background, then add more cobalt violet to the mix and strengthen the darks around the rocks, avoiding the very centre of the image. Still working wet-in-wet, add touches of a dark green mix – viridian, French ultramarine and burnt sienna – within the dark grey areas and allow to dry.

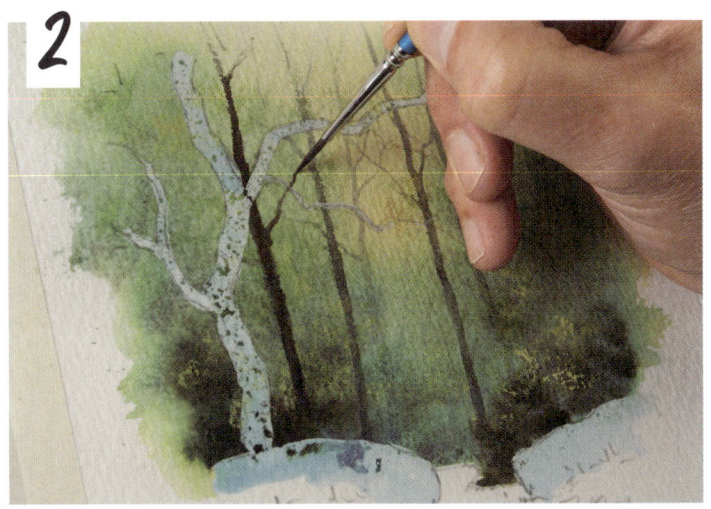

▶ Once dry, use the size 6 brush with the dry brush technique to apply the bright green mix and lemon yellow sparingly over the painting. This will break up the background and suggest the texture of the foliage. Allow the background to dry completely, then pick up a grey mix of cobalt blue, cobalt violet and burnt sienna with the size 2 round. Use this at different dilutions to add some simple background trees.

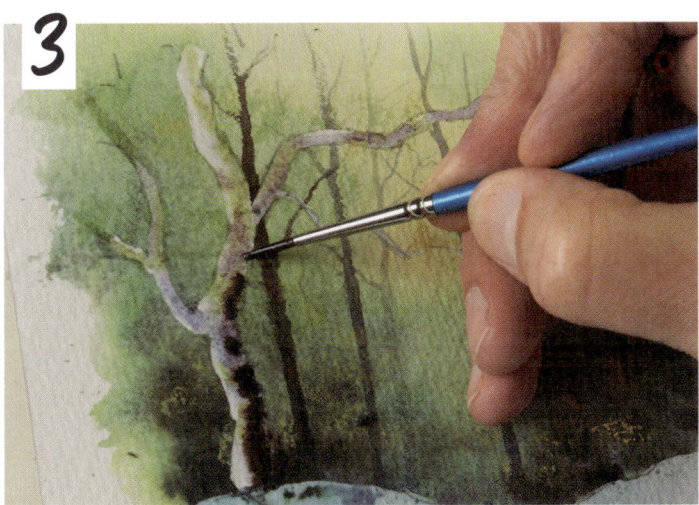

▶ Remove the masking fluid from the big tree on the left, but leave it in place on the rocks and water. Prepare a dark brown mix of burnt sienna and French ultramarine, and a shadow mix of cobalt blue and cobalt violet. Change to the size 4 brush and wet the revealed tree trunk and branches. Drop in some of the shadow mix, concentrating on the right-hand side. Touch in some of the bright green mix, then switch to a size 2 round and add some of the new dark brown, again concentrating on the right-hand side.

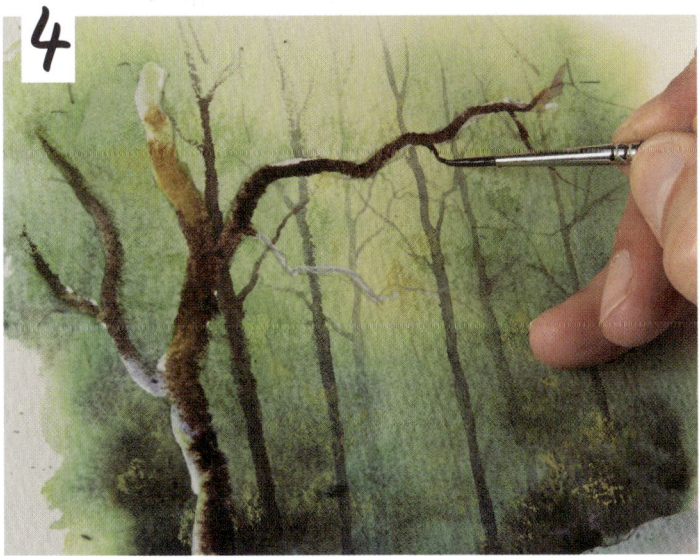

▶ Add a hint of lemon yellow wet-in-wet on the left-hand side, then use the dark brown mix to paint the finer branches.

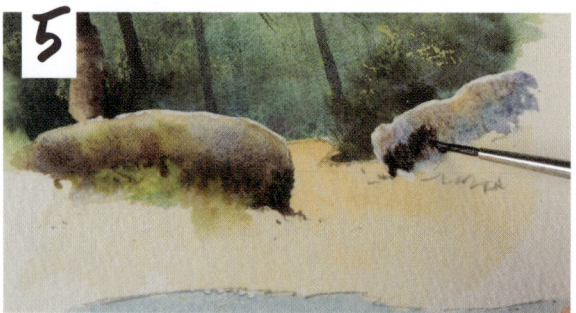

▶ Paint a thin wash of raw sienna on the path between the stones using the size 6 round brush, softening it down towards the river. Once dry, remove the masking fluid from the stones before using the size 4 round to wet the stone with clean water. Drop in raw sienna, leaving a thin line of white paper at the top, then add the shadow mix followed by the green-grey mix. While wet, add a mix of burnt sienna and French ultramarine to the lower part. Switch to the size 2 round brush and add a hint or two of lemon yellow to represent foreground grass in front of the rocks.

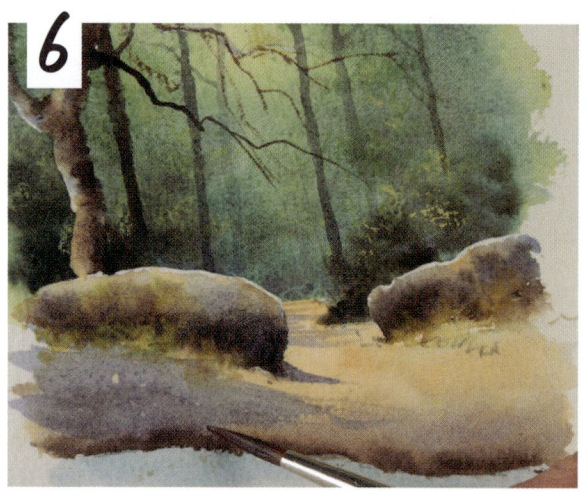

▶ Use the size 10 round to re-wet the path down to the water's edge, then drop in some raw sienna. Drop in some of the shadow mix with a size 6. Swap to a size 2 round brush and drop in some of the burnt sienna and French ultramarine mix on the very edge of the bank before adding more of the shadow mix across the path.

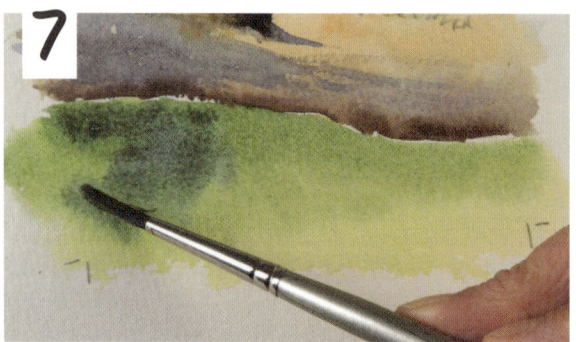

▶ Remove the remaining masking fluid. For the water, we will use a repetition of the colours used in the background, so refresh your mixes (see step 1). Wet the whole area, leaving a fine line of dry paper between the water and the bank. Drop in lemon yellow across the whole area with the size 10 round. Add the bright green mix wet-in-wet near the top. Next, change to the size 4 and add the green-grey mix, again nearer the bank. Use the size 6 to add some of the dark green mix as close to the edge as possible without going over the line of dry paper.

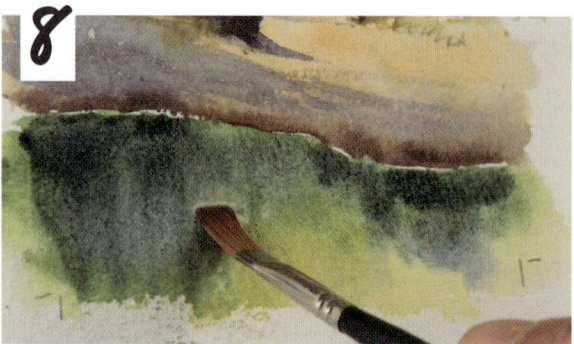

▶ Working wet-in-wet, add some of the shadow mix (cobalt violet and cobalt blue) in the water below the stones. Dampen a 6mm (¼in) flat brush and use it with a light flicking motion to draw the wet paint straight downwards from the bank to blend the colours vertically. Make sure the strokes are perpendicular to the bank.

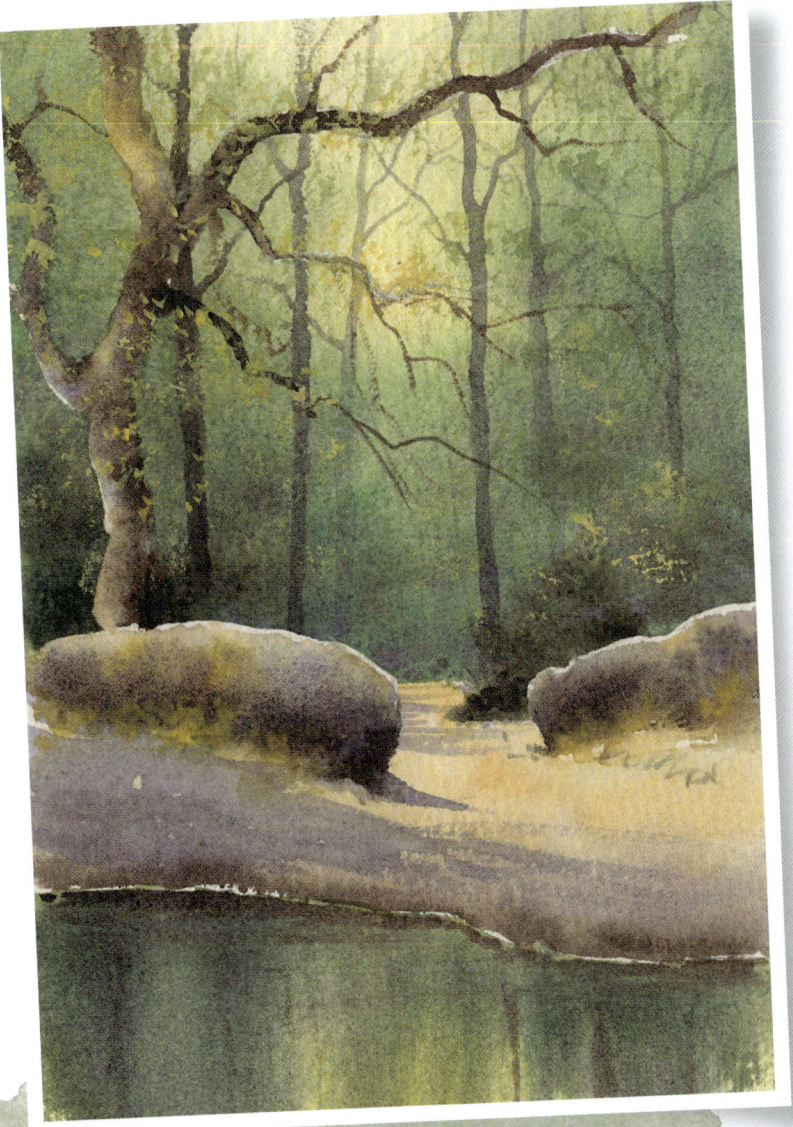

FINISHING TOUCHES

Use vertical strokes of a dilute cobalt blue, cobalt violet and burnt sienna mix to add reflections of the trees, then add a dark line that follows the edge of the water with the same brush and mix to finish off the painting perfectly.

Outline drawings

An outline drawing is provided for every postcard painting project in this book. If you don't feel confident enough to draw freehand, you can transfer the outline to your watercolour paper by following the simple steps below.

USING TRACEDOWN PAPER

This is an easily available paper for transferring images, sometimes known as graphite paper, and is similar to the carbon paper that was used in the days of typewriters.

1 Slip your sheet of watercolour paper directly under the outline you want to use.

2 Slip a sheet of tracedown paper between the outline and the watercolour paper. Go over the lines using a burnisher.

3 Remove the tracedown paper and lift up the outline to reveal the image transferred onto your watercolour paper, ready for you to begin painting.

USING PENCIL

You can transfer the outlines onto your watercolour paper using a pencil and a burnisher. If you prefer not to work directly from this book, you can photocopy or scan the outline first, and transfer the outline from a copy in much the same way.

1 Scribble over the back of the outline with a soft pencil.

2 Turn the page so that you are looking at the image you want to transfer. Place your watercolour paper underneath the page. Go over the lines with a burnisher.

3 Lift the page to reveal the image transferred onto your watercolour paper. When you remove the watercolour paper, make sure you put a piece of scrap paper in between this outline and the next to avoid graphite from the back of the drawing transferring onto the facing page.

SEND ANOTHER POSTCARD!

Copies of the outline drawings are available to download free from the Bookmarked Hub. Search for this book by title or ISBN: the files can be found under 'Book Extras'.

Membership of the Bookmarked online community is free: www.bookmarkedhub.com

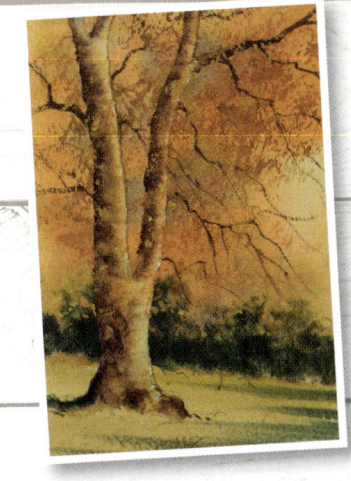

Autumn Tree 16

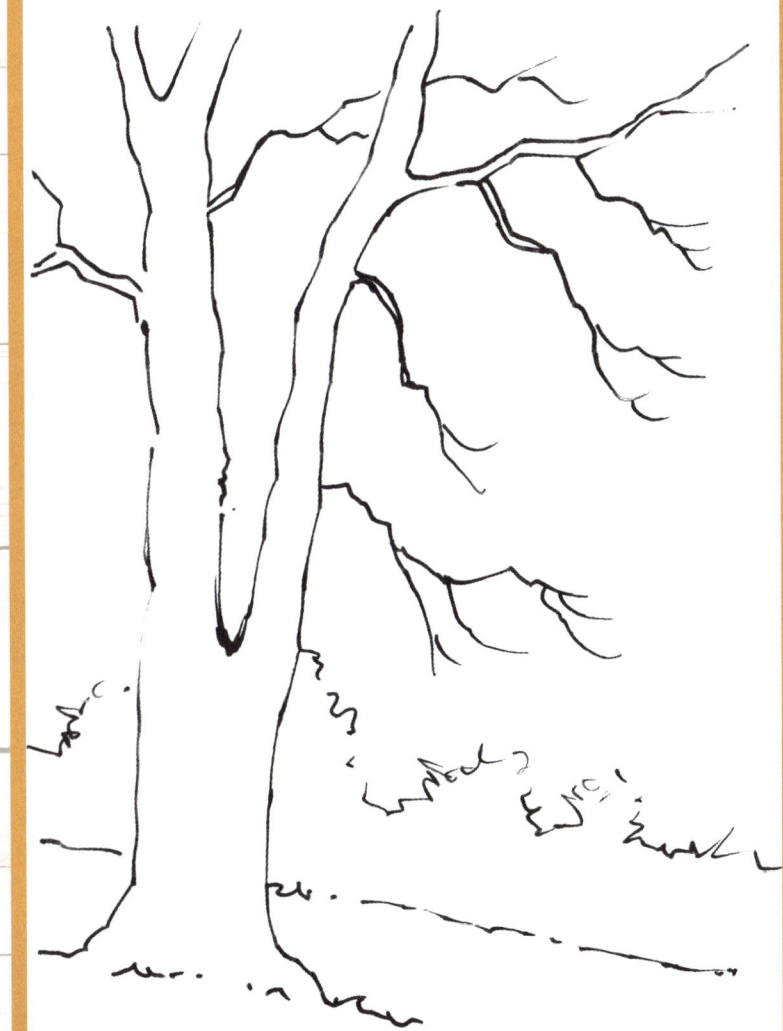

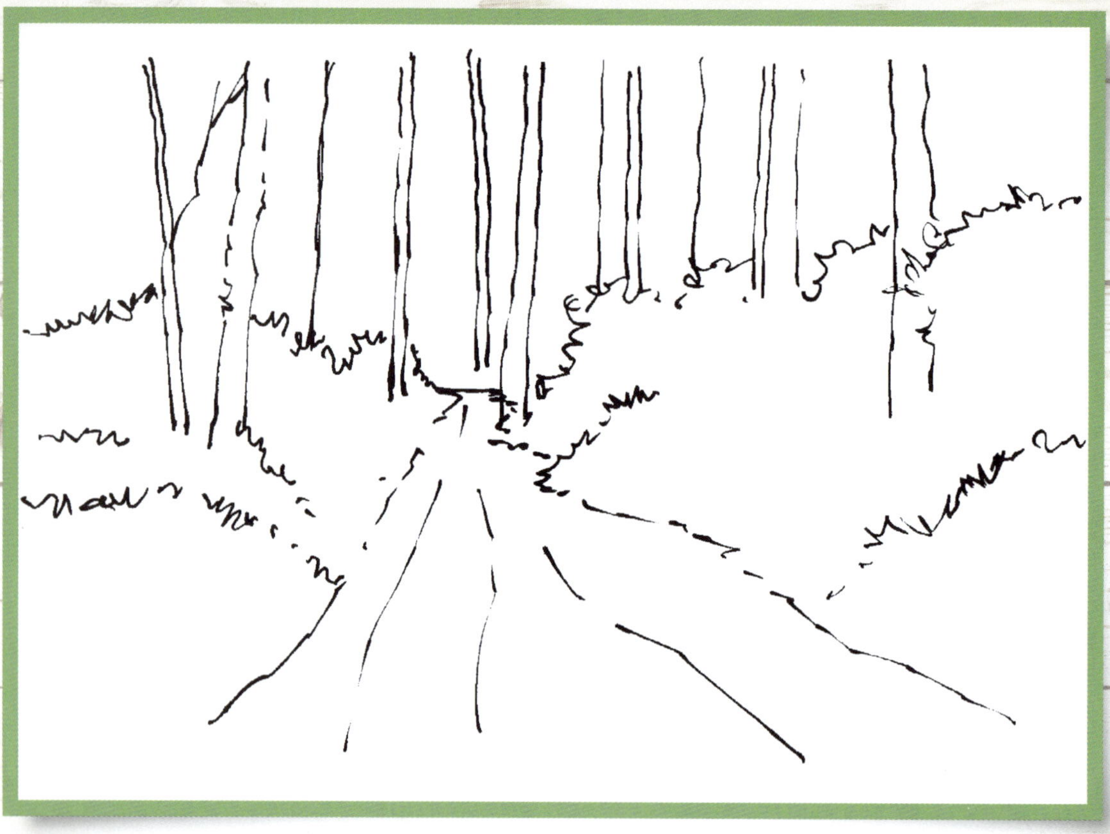

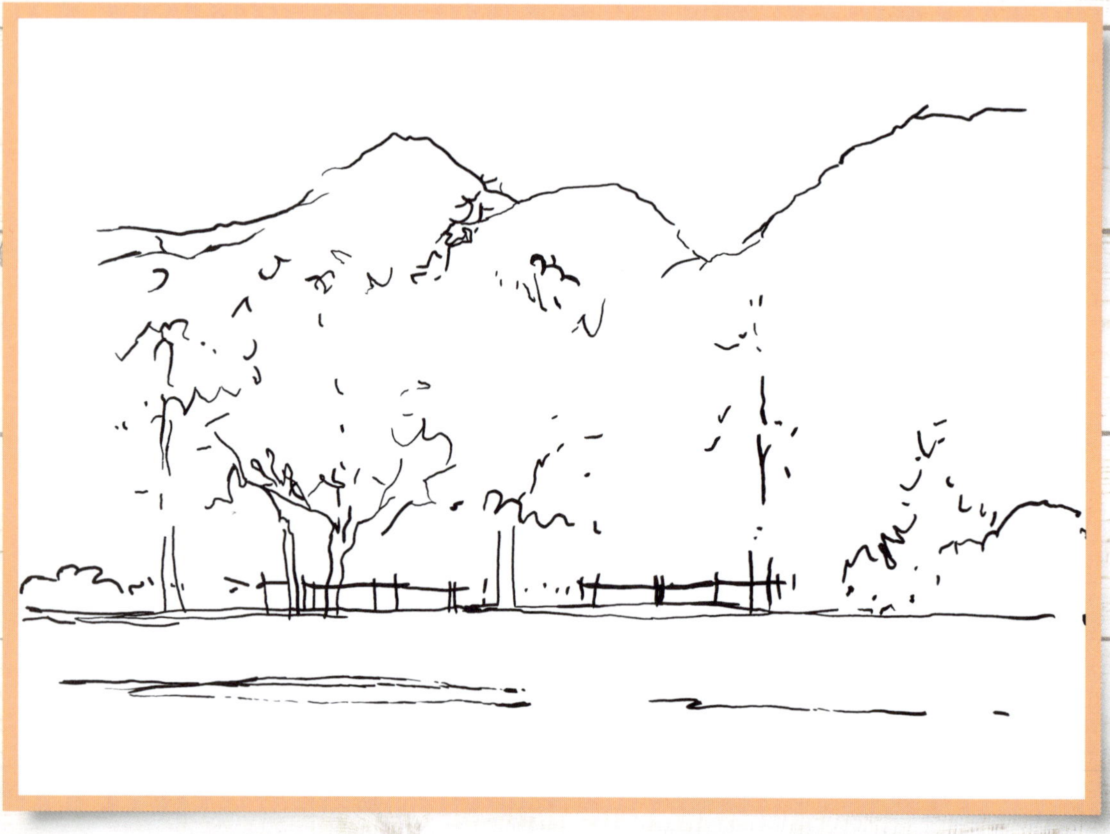

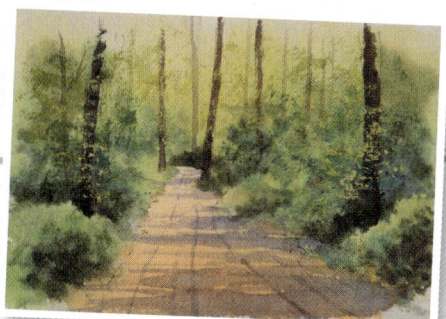

Spring Trees 22

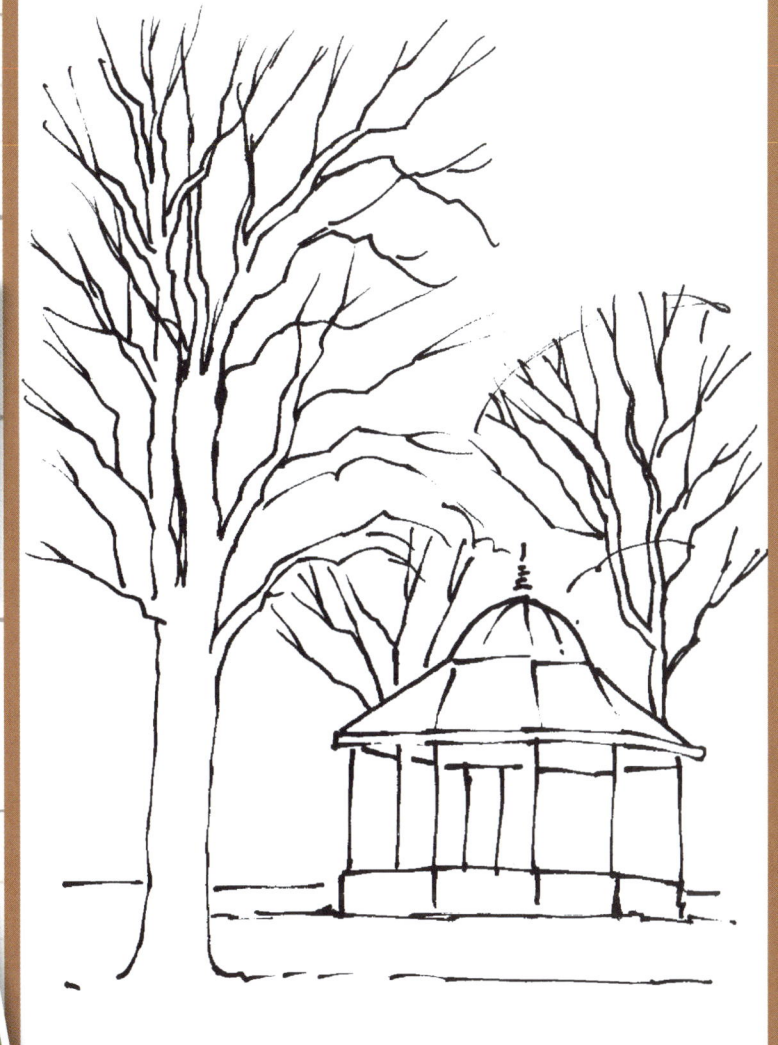

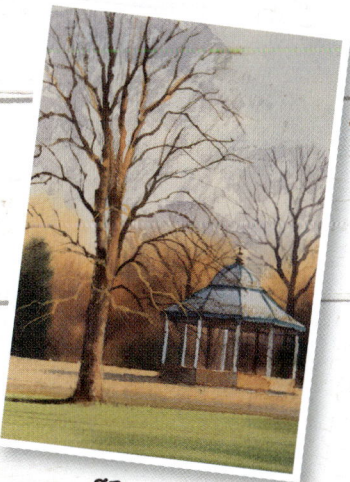

Summer Trees 28

Bandstand in the Park 32

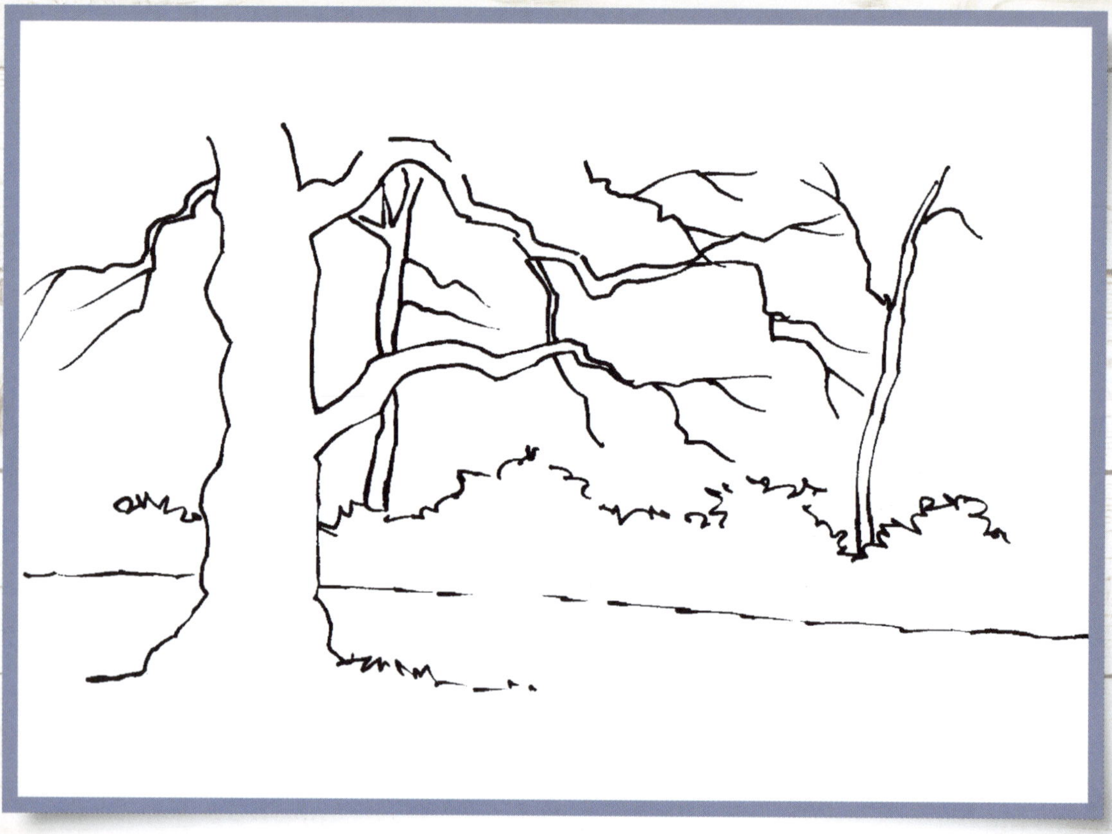

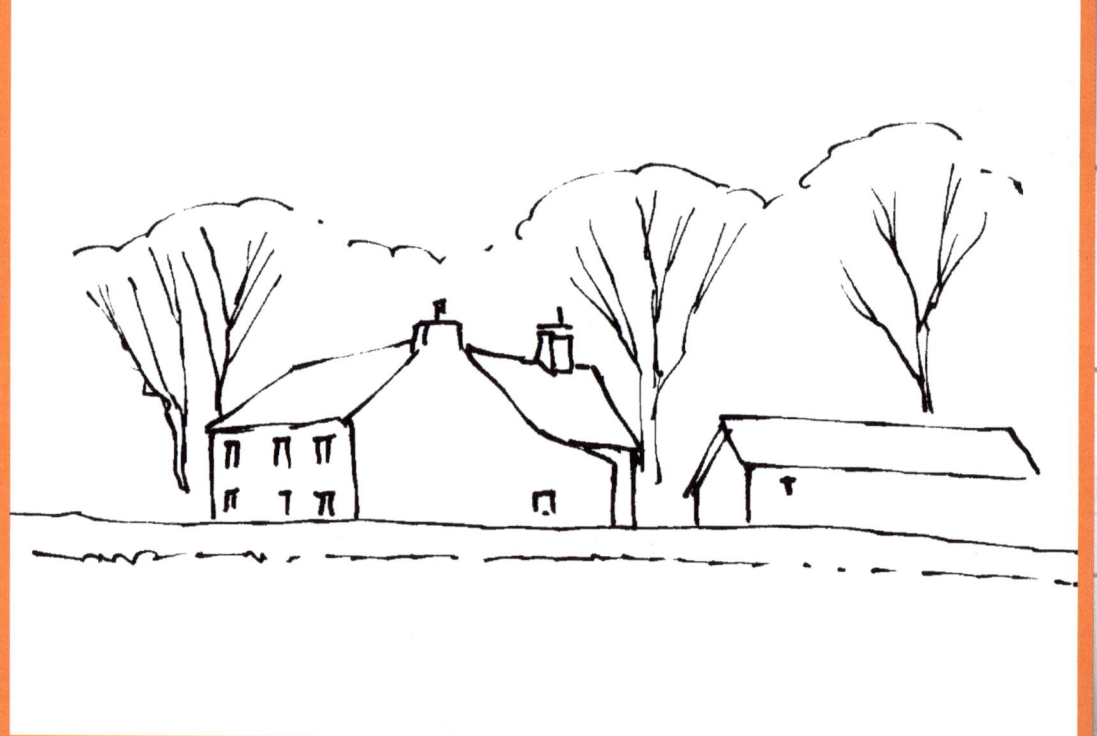

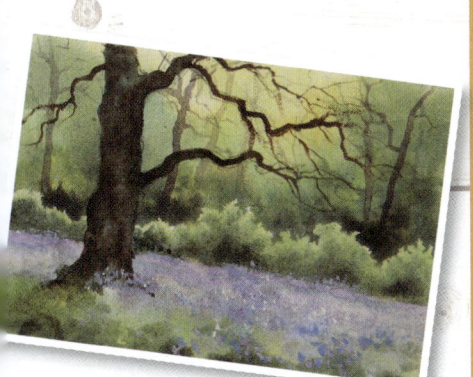

Bluebell Wood 36

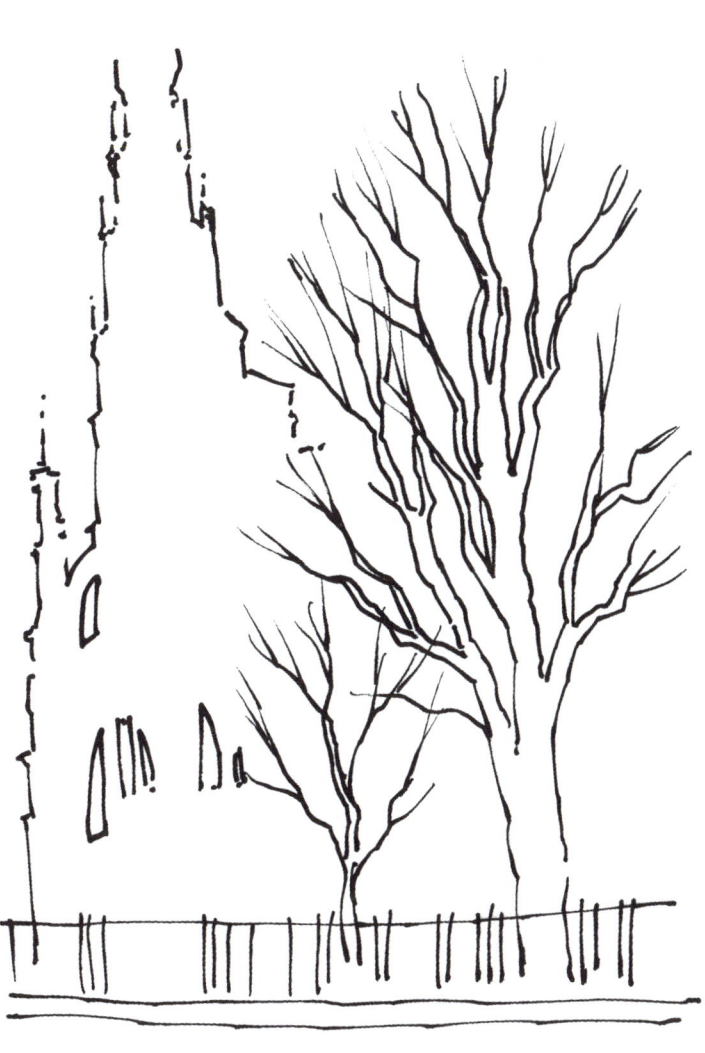

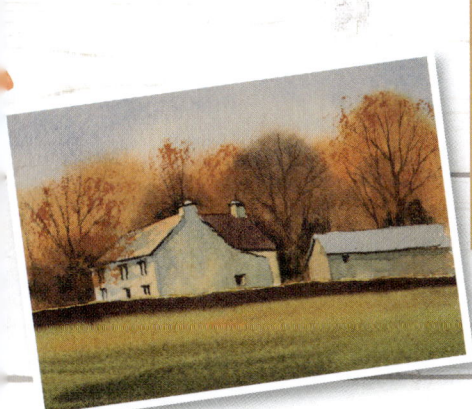

Farmhouse 40

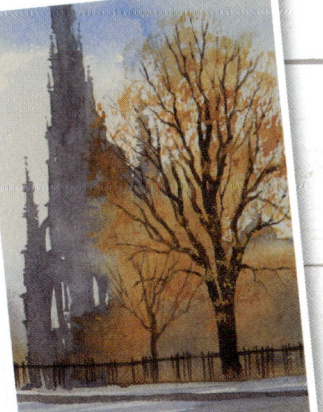

City Trees 44

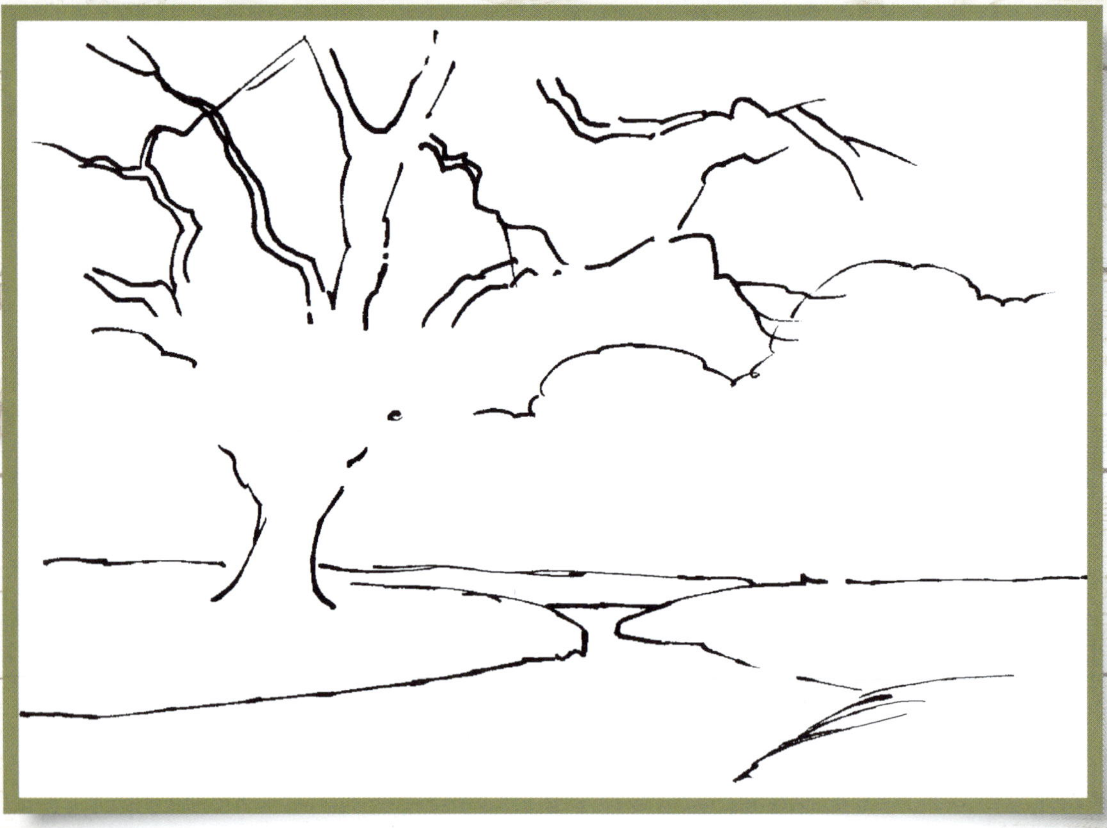

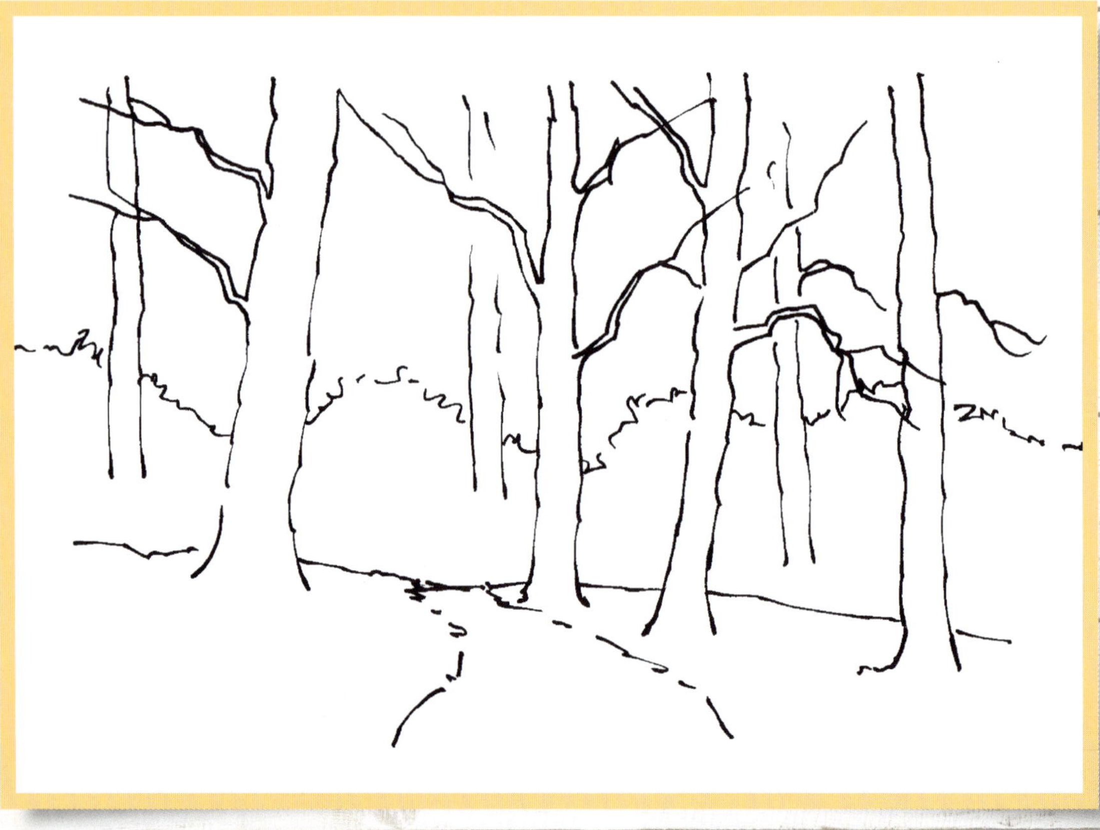

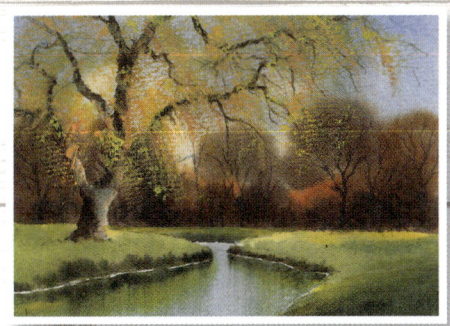

Weeping Willow 48

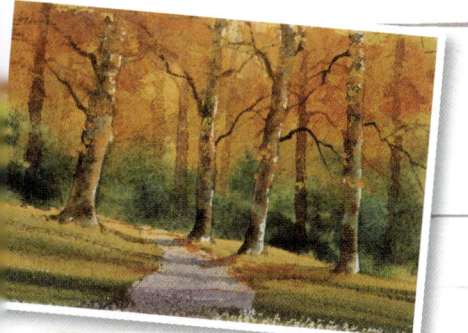

Parkland in Autumn 52

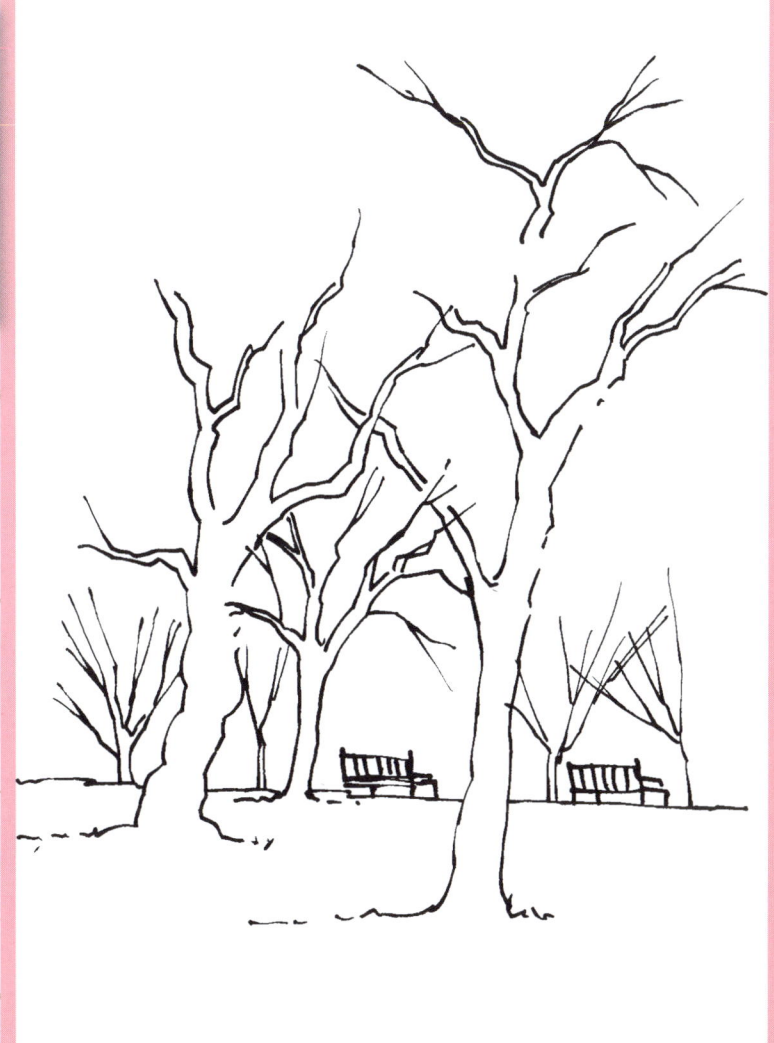

Cherry Blossom 56

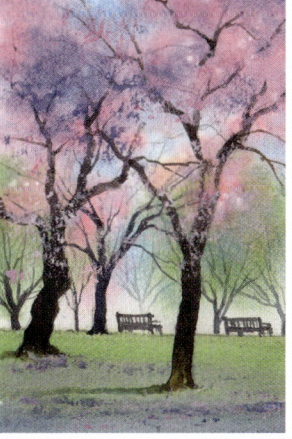

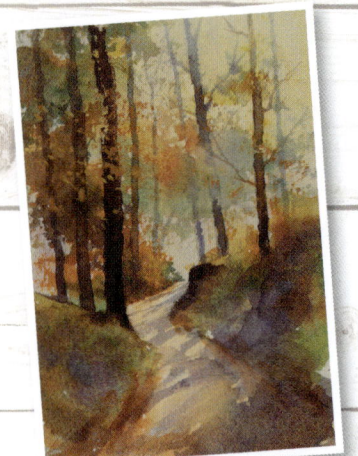

Dappled Sunlight 62

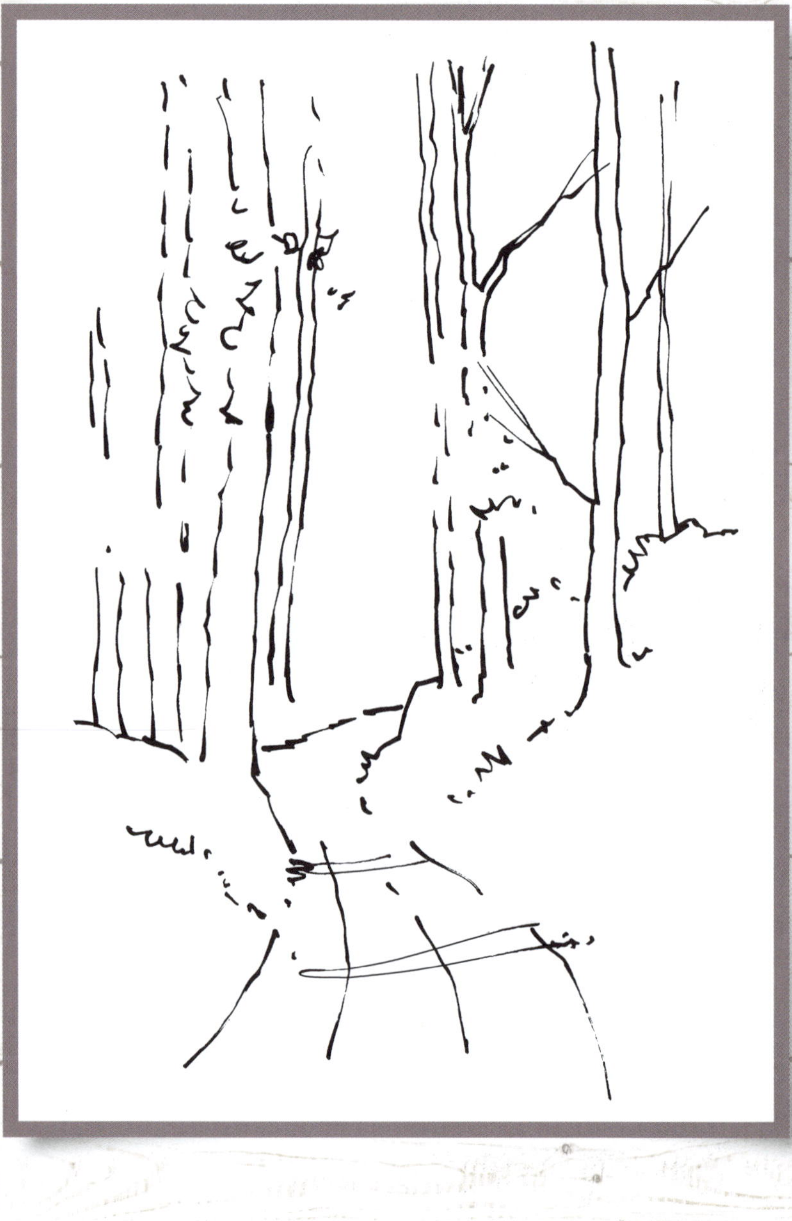

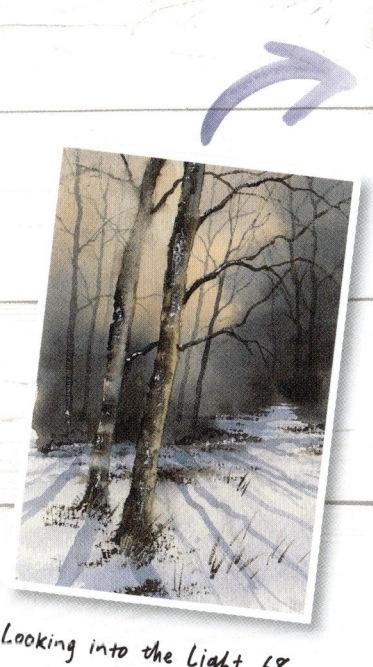

Looking into the Light 68

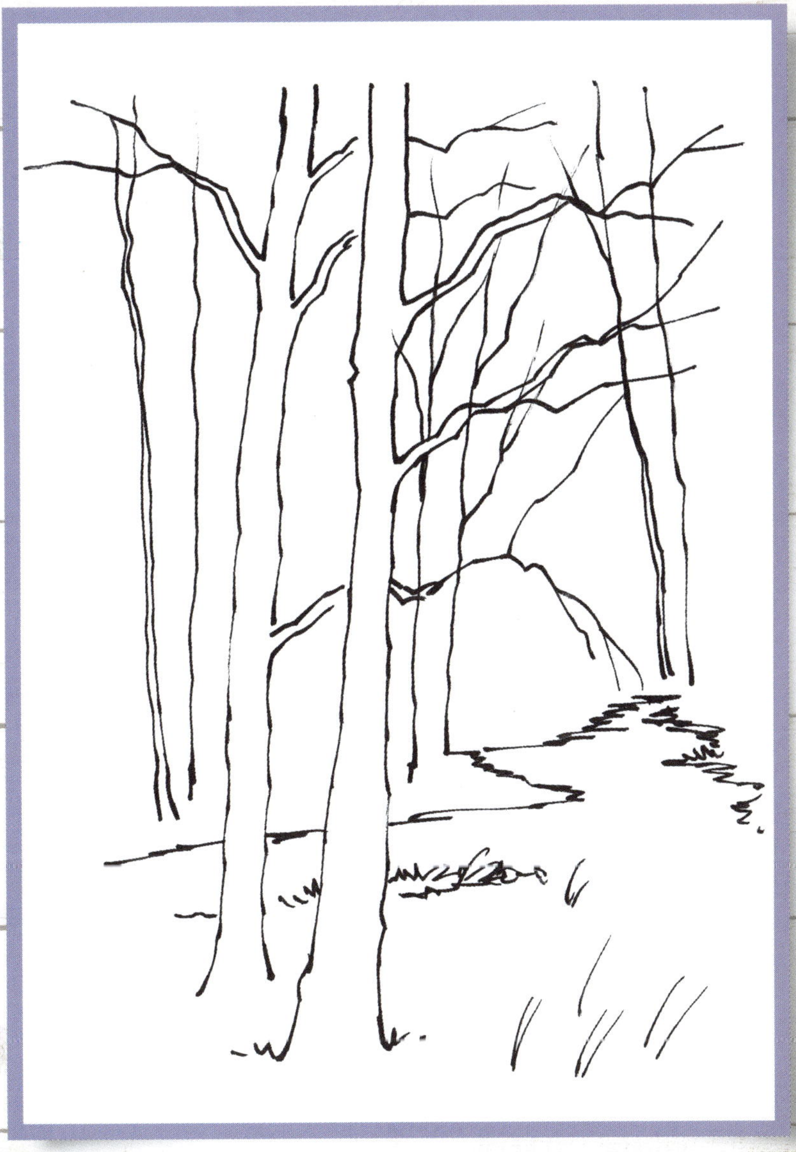

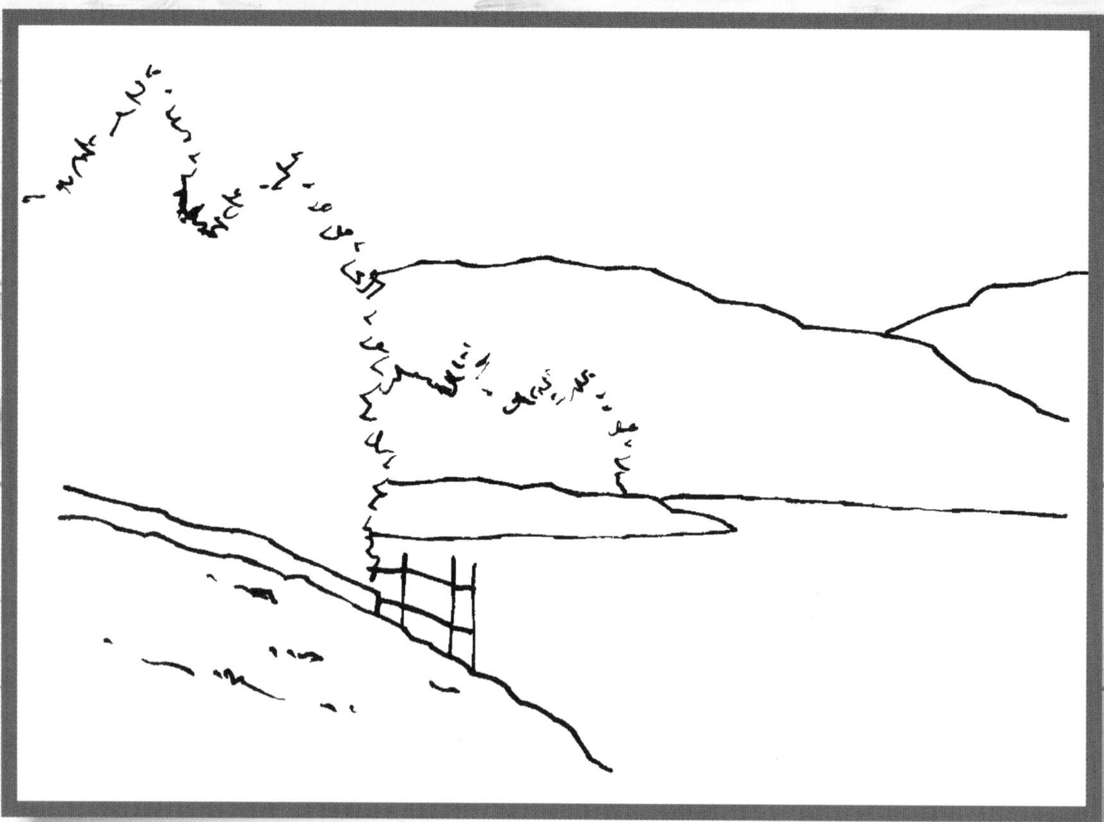

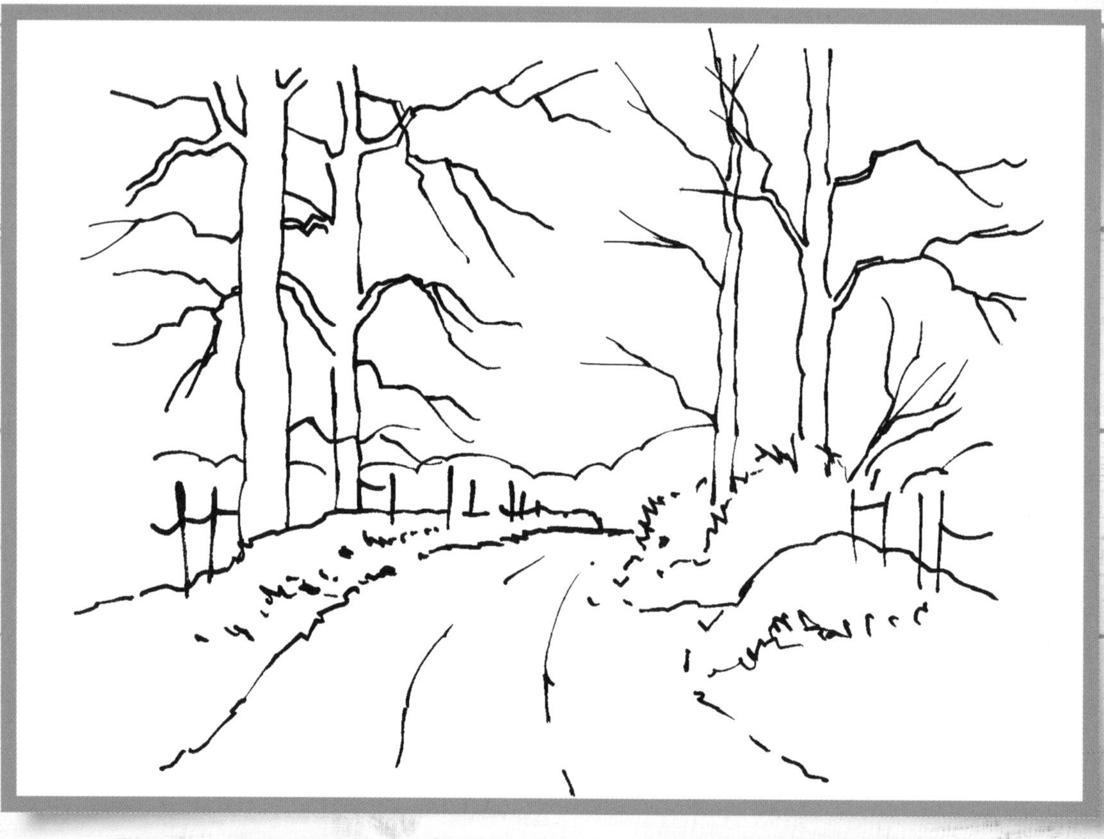

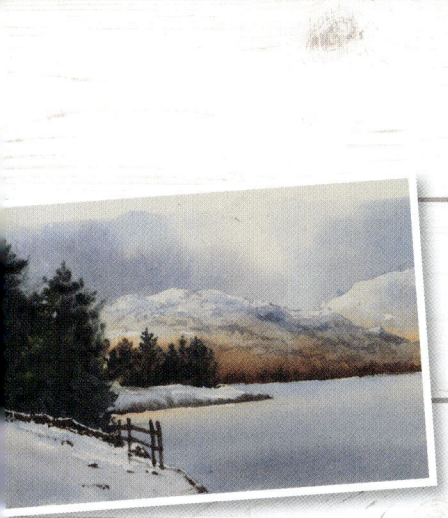

Fir Trees 72

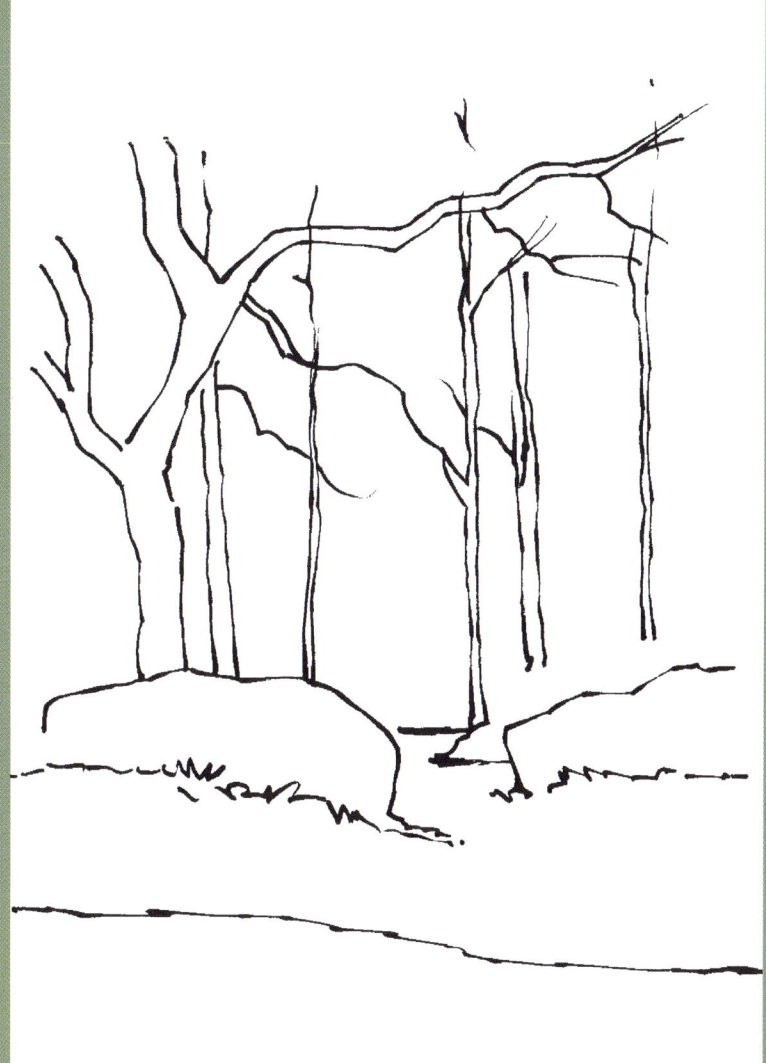

Winter Lane 76

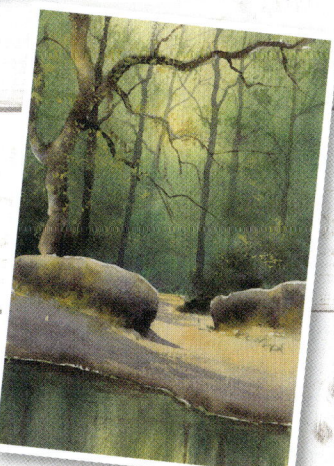

Pond Reflections 80

Index

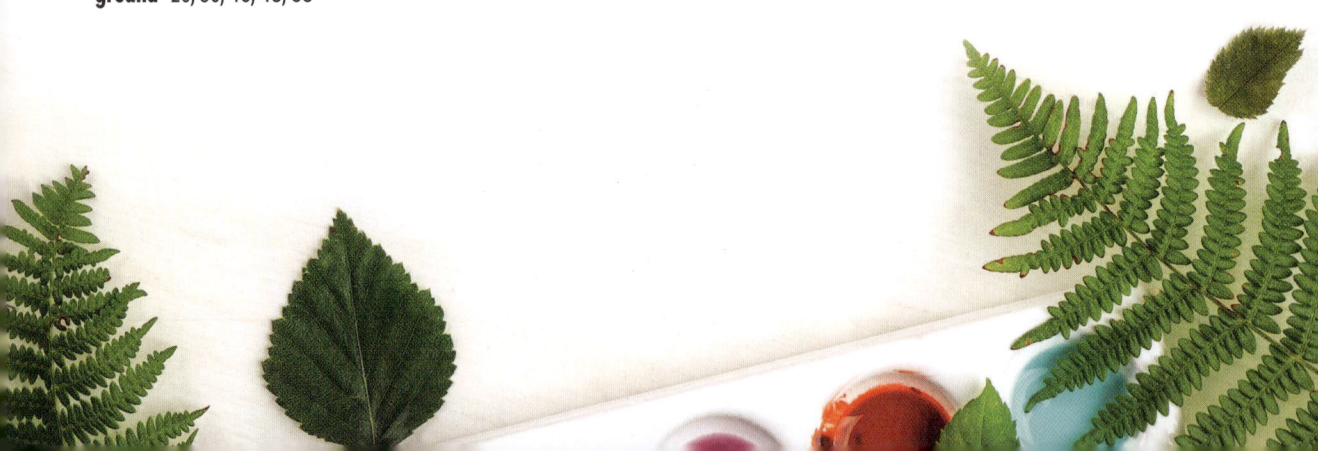